The Frog Princess

ANGIE BEASLEY

WITH MARIA MALONE

MICHAEL JOSEPH
an imprint of
PENGUIN BOOKS

MICHAEL JOSEPH

Published by the Penguin Group
Penguin Books Ltd, 80 Strand, London WC2R ORL, England
Penguin Group (USA) Inc., 375 Hudson Street, New York, New York 10014, USA
Penguin Group (Canada), 90 Eglinton Avenue East, Suite 700, Toronto, Ontario, Canada M4P 2Y3
(a division of Pearson Penguin Canada Inc.)
Penguin Ireland, 25 St Stephen's Green, Dublin 2, Ireland (a division of Penguin Books Ltd)
Penguin Group (Australia), 250 Camberwell Road, Camberwell, Victoria 3124, Australia
(a division of Pearson Australia Group Pty Ltd)
Penguin Books India Pvt Ltd, 11 Community Centre, Panchsheel Park, New Delhi – 110 017, India
Penguin Group (NZ), 67 Apollo Drive, Rosedale, Auckland 0632, New Zealand
(a division of Pearson New Zealand Ltd)
Penguin Books (South Africa) (Pty) Ltd, 24 Sturdee Avenue,
Rosebank, Johannesburg 2196, South Africa

Penguin Books Ltd, Registered Offices: 80 Strand, London WC2R ORL, England

www.penguin.com

First published 2011

1

Copyright © Angie Beasley and Maria Malone, 2011

The moral right of the authors has been asserted

For the protection and privacy of individuals concerned, some names and
identifying characteristics have been changed.

Printed in Great Britain by Clays Ltd, St Ives plc

A CIP catalogue record for this book is available from the British Library

ISBN: 978-0-718-15831-6

www.greenpenguin.co.uk

Penguin Books is committed to a sustainable
future for our business, our readers and our
planet. This book is made from paper certified
by the Forest Stewardship Council.

I

The air in the bedroom is cold. Freezing. I pull the blankets over my chin up to my nose and the wool tickles as I breathe. It's dark and I can't see much, just the bunched-up shape at the foot of the bed that's my dressing gown, and the chest of drawers against the far wall. It's quiet, not a sound coming from anywhere, as if there's only me here. It's never just me, though. There's always somebody else in the house. I lift the thick layer of blankets and slide out onto the rug at the side of the bed. I don't put my feet on the lino if I can help it because it feels cold, even through my woolly socks. Under my pyjamas I'm wearing a vest but as soon as I'm out of bed the snug feeling I had when I was under the covers goes and I huddle for warmth in my quilted dressing gown.

The landing is darker than my room and, opposite, the door to the bedroom where Mum and Dad sleep is shut. I go downstairs, the way they've taught me, first one foot on a step and then the next, taking my time, holding onto the wooden banister. The carpet is worn in the middle, almost to the bare wood underneath here and there. I make sure I don't trip.

Downstairs, I go into the front room where the curtains are open and it's lighter. I say his name: Trevor. I have to keep looking until I find my baby brother. I pad into the kitchen where it's cold, no kettle boiling on the stove. In the living room, the curtains are still shut and the light is on, making everything yellowy. Aunty Mabel kneels in front of the fire, getting it ready, tearing sheets of old newspaper and scrunching them into balls, pushing them into the gaps between the lumps of coal. She turns when I come in and gives me a big smile. 'Look at you, Angela – the early bird gets the worm,' she says. 'Come and give me a hand, then.'

She hands me a piece of newspaper and I make it into a ball like she does, and put it in the hearth. Aunty Mabel adds it to the ones already in the grate and strikes a match, touching the flame to all the little bits of paper poking out around the shiny black coals. She sits back, waiting for the fire to catch, and wipes her hands on a stringy cloth that's looped into the pocket of her housecoat. There's a damp patch on the nylon overall where the cloth has been. The fire burns and I kneel next to her liking the sudden heat, wishing it was warm like this in my bedroom where in the morning the windows have water running down the insides. One of the things I like best on cold nights is having my bath in the tin tub in front of the fire, Mum going in and out of the kitchen, pouring hot water from the kettle, adding in cold, until it's exactly the right temperature, steam seeping into the air as I get in. My night things are put to warm by the hearth and there's always a toasty towel waiting to dry me off when the water's going cold and it's time to get out.

Aunty Mabel takes a poker and jabs at the coals, sending sparks flying up the chimney, and puts up the fireguard. Through the black mesh of the metal guard the flames leap about while the coals shift and glow red.

I like her being here. Sometimes I stay with her round the corner from where we live in Buller Street, in Grimsby. Where she lives, a terraced house almost the same as ours, it's even colder than it is at home. I say, 'I can't find Trevor,' and she shuffles round so she's facing me instead of the fire. The heat has made her cheeks flushed and her hair, more grey than red, coarse and swept straight back, makes the lines on her face deeper, more severe. She is Mum's aunty, really, older than my other aunties, the same sort of age as my nana. She takes my hands and gives them a rub. 'Shall we get some breakfast?'

What I really want is to find my little brother. I keep looking for him, searching the place top to bottom. 'Where's Trevor?'

Aunty Mabel doesn't answer. She does up the buttons on my dressing gown, straightens the collar and gets to her feet, using the mantelpiece to pull herself up.

'Old bones,' she says, giving her knees a rub. She takes my hand again and steers me away from the fire and into the kitchen.

Everything I think I know about what happened to Trevor, all the memories I have, are from scraps of information given to me by other people – a drip-drip of bits and pieces over the years. That night, Aunty Mabel put me to bed. Mum was working the six to ten shift at the factory on the docks down the road. She came in from work and went straight upstairs to check on Trevor, who was eleven months old, and in his cot in her and Dad's room. Downstairs, Aunty Mabel stoked the fire, keeping the room cosy. My mum would be cold from packing frozen food on the production line and from coming in at that time of night.

Mum's screams filled the house. Aunty Mabel ran to the foot of the stairs and saw Mum on the landing at the top, her face twisted in pain, a dreadful sound coming from her. She had Trevor's still body in her arms.

Dad was on night shift at the docks and someone ran the half mile through quiet streets past houses mostly in darkness with curtains drawn to fetch him. I was scooped out of bed and taken to Mrs Pert next door. An ambulance turned into Buller Street and stopped outside our house, two wheels up on the narrow pavement, its blue light winking through the window. Over the road some of the neighbours came out and stood in front of their open front doors, arms crossed, white-faced, all eyes on our house. Mrs Pert, with her kind face, her grey hair in curlers, made me a hot milky drink and tucked a blanket round my legs. The blue light of the ambulance blinked on and off until finally the engine started up and it pulled away.

Every day afterwards the house was full of visitors – Nana and Aunty Janet and Uncle Colin and people I didn't know, drinking cups of tea and talking in low voices, wiping their faces with hankies, whispering about Trevor, saying how terrible it was, how tragic, that there was nothing anyone could have done.

I thought maybe Trevor was lost and that if I looked hard enough I'd find him. It was November 1966, and I was only three and a half, just a couple of years older than him, but I was his big sister and I loved him. It didn't make sense that he wasn't there any more, laughing and making his funny little noises and fastening his arms round my neck. I was just about big enough to pick him up and give him a proper cuddle. I kept on at Aunty Mabel asking about him and she'd hug me and make a fuss and take me to stay at her house so Mum could lie down, but she never did tell me where he was.

Mum never spoke to me about Trevor. It was too painful. On the night he died she had gone to work and everything at home had been fine, then, without warning, while she packed fish on a production line, her sleeping child had stopped breathing. Cot death. There wasn't a thing anyone could do.

2

Once a week a big red-faced woman trundled down Buller Street on a three-wheeler bike pulling a rickety trailer, ringing a small silver bell on the handlebars. She was the comic lady in a heavy tweed overcoat that looked at least a size too small and thick tan stockings that wouldn't stay up and sagged in wrinkles round her ankles. On her head she had a paisley-print scarf done up like a turban knotted at the front that didn't quite manage to cover the rollers she always had in. A few stray brown curls, damp from her efforts on the bike, always seemed to escape from the side of her scarf and end up plastered to her cheeks.

I used to get *Twinkle* and *Bunty*. I liked *Bunty* best because every week there was a doll on the back and a whole set of clothes you could cut out and dress her up in. I'd sit at the table with a pair of scissors with rounded ends, cutting out the blonde-haired figure, trying out different outfits that had little white tabs you used to keep them on. If you made a mess when you were doing the cutting-out and sliced off the tabs you'd had it – they were all that held the clothes up.

With Trevor gone, the house was quiet. Aunty Mabel or Aunty Janet looked after me because Mum was poorly and couldn't get out of bed. I had a new friend now, Katy, who came everywhere with me. She was like my shadow. We did everything together. The strange thing was that nobody else could see her and, sometimes, if we were playing with our dolls on the floor and Aunty Mabel came in she would almost stand on her. I'd have to tell her to watch out and Aunty Mabel would stop in her tracks and give me a knowing little smile. I always had to remind her to set an extra place for Katy at the table, too. I could never work out why I was the only one who knew she was there. She was real enough to me.

If it was a nice day I'd play out. I'd go into the back garden and ride my bike up and down the passage that ran behind the houses. I had a three-wheeler, like the one the comic lady rode, except mine didn't have a bell. A few doors along from us was my best friend, Steven. Up and down I'd go, gathering speed, freewheeling with my feet off the pedals and my legs stuck out at the sides, shouting for him at the top of my voice: 'STEEE-VEN!' I loved the wind in my face and how it blew my hair about as I gathered speed, waiting for him to come out and shout back – 'ANNN-GELA!' His back gate would fly open and we'd be off, riding our bikes to the end of the passage, doing on your marks, get set, go, and pedalling like mad all the way back again. It felt like we went miles. Sometimes I was laughing so much I nearly tipped the bike over.

I had stopped going on at Aunty Mabel about Trevor and no longer searched the place for him. I knew he wasn't there. When I did think about him I couldn't remember exactly what he looked like any more. Everything to do with Trevor was starting to get a bit blurry. I'd had my picture taken with him lots of times but I didn't know what had happened to the photographs. They weren't on the sideboard or the mantelpiece in the living room where the other pictures of me and Mum and Dad were. Mum would know where they were but I didn't like to ask. She was so ill she needed to sleep a lot and something had happened to her legs that meant she couldn't manage to get downstairs. I didn't know what was wrong with her, not really, just that it was to do with what had happened to Trevor.

I sat at the table trying different outfits on Bunty. Her hair was fastened with a big red bow and she had one hand under her chin and the other by her side. I picked out a short green dress with buttons down the front and a big white floppy collar. There were tabs at the shoulder and waist to keep it on but it kept slipping off. A yellow jumper with a shawl collar and a pair of red tartan trousers stayed on better. I held her up. Bunty had tons of lovely clothes – dresses, and little flared skirts and tops, and coats with nipped-in waists and shiny buttons. There were even matching-coloured shoes and socks.

At the front door, Aunty Mabel stood for a long time talking to someone I couldn't see. When she finally came in she had some papers in her hand and asked me to run to the shop on the corner while she popped up to see Mum. She jotted down a list, took a string bag from a hook on the back of the kitchen door, and said to tell the lady to put it all on account and she'd settle up at the end of the week. I felt like a proper big girl going to the shop on my own when I was only just four. I did a hop, skip and a jump as I went down the street. Up ahead, a few doors along from us, two women knocked on a door. A woman in a hairnet with a little girl balanced on her hip answered, and went to shut the door straight away until one of the women on the pavement put up a hand to stop her and took what looked like a magazine from her bag. I was almost level with them and the woman with the little girl was shaking her head and saying, 'I've got my own religion, thanks,' as she shut the door.

Over my shoulder, I saw the women move on and knock at the next house.

3

Mum fastened my duffel coat up to the neck, looped a scarf under my chin, and helped me into the red woollen mittens that hung on a piece of elastic threaded through my sleeves. We walked along Buller Street, Mum in her big coat and a pair of stout black boots with a furry lining, me slipping a hand out of its glove and flinging my arm up and down, watching the mitten dance about. It was December 1967.

'That wind's straight off the sea,' Mum said, shivering and putting her head down, burrowing into her collar.

The bitter wind stung my face and when I touched my cheek it felt frozen. I put the mitten back on. We turned into Pasture Street, me jumping and skipping over the faded outline of hopscotch squares chalked onto the ground, almost losing my balance, hanging onto Mum's hand.

She tugged me upright. 'Angela, you'll have me over if you're not careful.'

I glanced up at her. The thing was, you couldn't just walk all over a hopscotch grid – everybody knew that. I took an extra long step so as not to put my foot on a join in the pavement. Mum kept walking, seeming not to care that she was standing on cracks right, left and centre. Inside the hood of my duffel coat I pulled a face. Maybe it didn't matter about stuff like that once you got big.

We turned into Edward Street. Lights blazed from the windows of the school and children streamed across the playground, disappearing inside. The building, with its long windows and high, jagged roof seemed massive to me. At the gate, Mum bent to give me a kiss.

'Ooh, you're frozen,' she said, pressing her face against mine and hugging me.

I blew into the air and my breath turned white. The school towered above me. I said, 'Why did they make it so big when all the girls and boys are little?'

She straightened up and looked as though she was thinking really hard. 'Well, what about the teachers?' She gave me a smile. 'They need a proper big place or they'd be bumping their heads all the time.' I opened my mouth to say something but Mum said, 'Now, in you go, and no more daft questions.'

I ran across the playground, shaking off my gloves and turning to wave with both hands. The mittens bounced up and down. She reached through the railings and waved back. Her gloves were black like her boots, with fingers and no elastic to make sure she didn't lose them.

Behind the double doors, huddled in the entrance in a smart checked coat, arms folded across her middle, was my class teacher, Mrs Laidlaw. Her dark hair was straight and framed her face. I wiped my feet on the mat, a stiff, scratchy thing fixed into a well in the floor. Our mat at home was just like it but you could pick ours up and give it a good shake outside. All kinds of stuff came out, dust flying everywhere when Mum beat it against the wall at the back. It made me wonder how they ever got the one at school clean.

'No running in the corridor, Angela,' Mrs Laidlaw said, the words making shapes in the chilly air.

'No, Miss.'

She hugged herself against the cold and looked at me for a moment as if she was about to say something else. I put my hood down and struggled with the toggle at my throat. Two deep lines appeared in the centre of Mrs Laidlaw's brow. 'Go and hang your coat up,' she said eventually, her voice sharp. 'And *no running.*'

The floor was shiny, polished-looking, and if I dragged my feet the soles of my shoes squeaked on the lino. I only did it once on the way to class, in case a teacher saw and told me off. You could get in trouble for all sorts, like hanging your coat on the wrong peg in the cloakroom or not putting your hand up in class before you spoke. Everyone else in my class was older than me and seemed to know the rules: what you were meant to do and what you definitely weren't. I'd heard Mum talking to Aunty Mabel, saying I shouldn't really have started school until the next year, but it was the best thing, what with all that had happened.

Along the corridor paper chains were pinned to the walls, some criss-crossing below the ceiling. One of the other classes had made them, cutting up strips of crêpe paper in red and green and white. There were pictures running the length of one wall: snowmen with beady button eyes and big round bodies covered in cotton wool, trees with bright, glittery baubles, and a robin with a fuzzy red breast made from felt. Gold tinsel framed the whole thing. Mrs Laidlaw said we had to call it a frieze. She wrote it on the board for us – F-R-I-E-Z-E – and I copied it into my book in my best writing. Mine looked a bit wonky and not as neat as hers did on the board.

At the front of the class, Mrs Laidlaw stood straight-backed, a fresh piece of chalk in one hand, smiling without showing her teeth. There was a bit of fidgeting going on, someone dragging a chair closer to their desk. She waited for silence.

'Sit up straight, please,' she said, and there was a shuffling as everyone did as they were told. I crossed my arms and rested them on the desk, shoulders back, chin up, eyes fixed on the board. It was still up there: F-R-I-E-Z-E.

Mrs Laidlaw put down her piece of chalk on the little ledge that ran the length of the blackboard. The front of her navy skirt had dust on it. She stepped to the side of her desk.

'Who can tell me what today is?' she said.

Silence.

'Come on, now. It's a very special day and we won't be having our usual lessons.' Several hands shot up, everybody straining to get theirs higher than the others. 'That's better.' Mrs Laidlaw surveyed the room. One or two of the girls were hissing, 'Miss, Miss.' She took no notice. 'Peter,' she said, picking a boy with glasses in the front row. 'You tell me. What's special about today?'

'We're having our party, Miss.'

'That's right. We're having our party.'

A burst of chatter went round the room. Janet, who sat beside me and had freckles and red hair done up in plaits, gave me a big smile and bounced about in her seat, the plaits doing a jig. I beamed back and nudged her with my elbow, getting excited.

Mrs Laidlaw clapped her hands twice to restore order. She was looking straight at me.

'Angela, will you come out here, please.'

I stayed put, sure she couldn't really mean for me to go to the front, even though I was the only Angela in the class. She crooked a finger. 'Yes, you, Angela Chapman,' she said. 'Out here – now, please.'

Janet was giving me a funny look. I got out of my seat.

Mrs Laidlaw took me by the shoulders and turned me to face everyone. They were all staring, the ones at the back leaning sideways out of their chairs to get a better look. Maybe I was going to get a telling off for running in the playground. I swallowed, wishing I was back in my seat, two rows from the front, smiling at Janet and her plaits. I stared at the floor.

'As you all know, today we're having our Christmas party,' Mrs Laidlaw said, 'and Angela is not allowed to join in.' She paused and I looked up. The faces in front of me were serious now, puzzled.

'The reason Angela cannot join in is . . .' Another pause. 'Well, perhaps she'd like to tell us.' I stood examining my shoes, brown lace-ups with a pattern made from holes punched into the leather. Brogues, my dad called them. I could fasten the laces on my own. Mrs Laidlaw had stopped speaking. She dug a finger into my shoulder and said, 'Angela, would you like to tell the class why you can't join in the Christmas party?'

My face burned, my mind was blank. I couldn't speak. Seconds ticked by.

She said, 'Angela is a *Jehovah's Witness*. Who knows what that is?'

Not a single hand went up.

'Can *you* tell us, Angela?'

My mouth was dry. Mum had told me we were Witnesses now and we went to meetings but I didn't really know what it meant.

Mrs Laidlaw's voice got louder. 'I'll tell, you, shall I?'

I clasped my hands behind my back and kept my eyes down. My shoes shone. Mum had polished them, spread a sheet of newspaper on the kitchen floor, taken waxy brown polish from a little round tin and rubbed it into the leather with an old yellow duster, waiting a few minutes before brushing them and making them look like new. I loved the smell of shoe polish.

'Angela follows a religion that does not believe in Christmas.' There were horrified murmurs. 'That's right – she does not believe in celebrating the birth of Christ.' I wished the ground would open up and swallow me. She touched my shoulder again. 'That means no party for you, young lady.' She sounded pleased with herself. 'Now, just because *Angela* seems to think Christmas is some kind of *pagan festival*, that doesn't mean the *rest of us* can't enjoy it.'

I caught a flicker of relief in the eyes of my classmates, as if for one horrible moment they had thought the party was off – thanks to me.

'Angela will have to miss the fun, I'm afraid.' Mrs Laidlaw escorted me back to my desk. 'Pick up your chair and come with me,' she said.

I did as I was told and went back to the front of the class again. She angled the chair with its back to the class. 'Up you get,' she said, taking me by the elbow and hoisting me onto the chair. I was nearly as tall as her now. Her skin was powdery, the colour of a rich tea biscuit, and her thin lips were painted red. I could smell her scent, something light and lemony.

'You can stand up there and face the blackboard while the rest of us have our party,' she said.

Up close, I noticed the line along her jaw where the rich tea colour ended and, underneath, her neck, pale and creamy, like the milk we got at break.

We did used to have Christmas. I remembered once waking up and finding presents at the bottom of the bed and one of Dad's socks, all lumpy, stuffed with an apple and a couple of little oranges and nuts in their shells. They were walnuts, rock hard, and Dad had to use pliers to smash them open. I'd thrown back the covers and got out of bed and knelt beside the pile of presents wrapped in shiny coloured paper. I knew they meant that Santa had been. I'd gone to see him in Grimsby, sat on his knee and nodded when he'd asked if I'd been a good girl. His beard was as white as Dad's best shirt and soft, like my hair. He was bristly too, though, and when he put his head on one side and asked what I wanted Santa to bring I could see stray grey hairs poking out of his ears. He said as long as I was good I'd get everything I wanted for Christmas.

In my bedroom after Santa had been there was a box nearly as big as me done up with a ribbon. I turned it over and tore at the paper to see what was inside and found a doll with plump arms and legs wearing a romper suit and bib trimmed in pink. Her eyes were bright blue, almost the same colour as my dad's. I opened the box and took her out, rocking her on my knee while her eyes opened and closed. She had lovely long sooty eyelashes that curled at the end. I couldn't think of a name for her so I called her Dolly. I don't think I'd had her long when I got told off for burying her in the back garden. Mum was really upset with me. That was before the women with the magazines started coming to the house to see her. It was them talking to her that got her on her feet again. She said she'd never have got better otherwise. After they'd been the first few times she got up and got dressed and came downstairs. It was ages since she'd done that. I'd started to think she'd be in bed for ever. Aunty Mabel said that Mum getting well after she'd been poorly for six months, just through talking and saying prayers, was a miracle. You only had to look at her to see she was on the mend. I knew something bad had happened to make her ill in the first place but I couldn't remember what it was. Those women who did Mum the world of good were called Witnesses and it was because of them that we were Witnesses now. I didn't mind being a Witness if that meant Mum was going to be all right, but I still wasn't sure why we couldn't have Christmas any more.

I stared at the blackboard while behind me desks were pulled together and chairs scraped across the wooden floor to make space for party games. Maybe I'd not been a good girl, like Santa said, like I'd been the year before. Maybe that's why I was on the chair at the front while everybody else was having a party. The volume rose as Mrs Laidlaw told everyone to take a Christmas cracker and the room filled with pops and giggling. Out of the corner of my eye, on the side wall of the classroom I could see the display of Christmas cards everyone had made, a colourful collection covered in glued-on tissue paper and glitter. I had not made a card, I'd done a calendar instead. I remembered Mrs Laidlaw saying I wasn't allowed to do the card so I'd drawn a house – a square with four windows and a front door right in the middle. I gave it a garden with a big tree and smoke curling from the chimney. I made the roof grey and the walls like the ones at school only my house was a bright red like a fire engine, not grimy and blackened like Edward Street Primary. I made the front door blue and, because it was winter and everyone else seemed to be doing pictures with snow on their cards, I put a snowman with a carrot nose and a scarf round his neck under the tree. I gave him a black hat and a happy face with lots of teeth, then stuck a little calendar with all the months of the year at the bottom of the picture and slotted ribbon through the top so you could hang it up. I was going to take it home for Mum when we broke up.

I thought about the calendar while everyone else played musical chairs, and tears stung my eyes. If you had to stand on a chair at the front of the class facing the board you must have done something wrong. You must have been bad. My legs ached from standing up and I kept blinking to stop the tears from coming.

Behind me, Mrs Laidlaw said, 'Right, class, everybody in a circle, cross-legged on the floor – we're going to play pass the parcel.'

4

I was about six when we moved out of the house in Buller Street. My brother, David, was two and Mum was expecting another baby. I was glad to be going because deep down I sensed that something about the place meant we weren't happy there and we never would be. No one ever said as much, not to me anyway, but everybody knew the Buller Street house held bad memories. I hardly ever thought about the baby brother I'd once had and whose death had cast such a terrible shadow and I never asked about him. I just knew my parents couldn't wait to get away and make a fresh start somewhere else.

Not long before we moved, when the few possessions we had were being packed away, my dad went up into the loft and came down jubilant, dragging a stack of paintings into the front room. He had dust on him from rummaging around among the rafters. It was the first time he'd been up there since we moved in.

He called to my mum in the kitchen. 'Mo, come and see what I've found.' He could barely contain himself.

Mum came into the room drying her hands on a tea towel and watched as he used his sleeve to wipe layers of dust off an ornate gilt frame. 'I'm trying to get the kitchen packed up, Ron,' she said, frowning.

'Never mind that. I've only found a stash of Old Masters,' he said, delighted, turning one of the pictures round.

'Old rubbish, more like,' Mum said.

'I'm telling you, they're worth a bit, these.'

I went and stood a couple of feet in front of the painting he was examining. It was nearly as big as me and showed a field, bales of yellow hay piled onto carts, the sky streaked with clouds and turning a brilliant shade of orange.

Dad grinned. 'See, Angela, your dad's only gone and hit the jackpot!'

My eyes widened. 'Are we going to be rich?'

'Course we are!' His eyes shone as he got down on his knees and peered at the picture. 'Let's see if whoever did it put their name on it, shall we? We might even have a Turner here.' He gave me a wink. 'A whole load of Turners, eh, Angela? What do you think of that?' He flipped through the rest that were propped up against the settee. 'Who was it did all those country scenes – the really famous ones?' His brow creased in concentration.

Mum made a tut-tut sound and rolled her eyes at me. 'Hark at your dad – thinks he's Picasso all of a sudden.'

'You won't be laughing when I sell them and make a fortune. Here, pass that tea towel.' He started wiping dust and cobwebs off the frames. 'Get another cloth and give us a hand, Angela.'

'For heavens sake, use a duster,' Mum said, exasperated. 'Get an old one from under the sink.' She sat on the edge of the settee while Dad checked the paintings, front and back for any sign of who might have done them.

'They didn't always sign them, did they?' he said. 'Sometimes the name would be painted over. I bet someone who knows their stuff could tell you straight away who did these.'

Mum was starting to show a bit more interest. 'We'll have to get them looked at.'

Dad gazed up at her. 'I'll take them in to the auction place or somewhere, get someone to value them,' he said.

I hopped from one foot to another. We were really going to be rich. I thought about the new house, which I'd not yet seen. I could have a bedroom all to myself, done out in pink, with floaty curtains and one of those four-poster beds, like the one in 'The Princess and the Pea'. Maybe we'd even get a different house now, something bigger – a mansion – once my dad sold the paintings and made a fortune.

He got to his feet and twirled my mum around. 'We're in the money,' he sang, 'we're in the money!'

Mum let him waltz her round the tiny room in her housecoat and slippers. 'Mind the paintings!' he said, swinging her about.

She shook with laughter. 'You daft thing, getting carried away when it's probably just a heap of junk.'

Days went by and I didn't dare ask about the paintings. I just waited for my dad to say we were rolling in it and I could go ahead and choose a bed fit for a princess. He never did, though. Mum turned out to be right. The pictures weren't worth anything.

The new house in Felstead Road was terraced, liked the old one, but there was more room and it was brighter, more modern. Downstairs, we had gas fires instead of the coal ones we'd been used to. Best of all, at the back of us were fields that seemed to go on for ever. There were lots of other children in the street; a big family next door and a blond lad over the road, Steven, who I got friendly with. If it was a nice day we were always out, building dens and running about in the long grass pretending to be soldiers or cowboys and Indians. I'd be gone for hours at a time. At home, Mum had her hands full with David, who seemed happy trailing along behind her while she cleaned and cooked, and there was a new baby too, my brother Ian. The washer was always going and she was in and out pegging nappies and tiny vests and all-in-ones on the line in the back garden, getting one lot dry as the next ones came out of the machine. She never seemed to sit down for five minutes and put her feet up. She'd pour a cup of tea, get distracted, and find it cold, forming a ring on the cup, and end up tipping it down the sink. I was the eldest and I didn't need telling that I had to muck in and do my bit and – just as important – keep out from under her feet, too. Getting on with things and making my own entertainment was second nature and it was probably a relief to Mum that she never had to worry about what I was up to. Even if nobody else was playing out I'd tramp across the fields, imagining I was going to a special secret place where anything could happen. I could while away hours sitting in the ditch that was our den, lost in my own little world.

Mum handed me a plate with a slice of thin white bread toasted and cut in half, the margarine melting and running across the surface. I added a thick layer of strawberry jam.

She stirred something on the stove. 'Do you want another slice?'

I nodded. Jam dripped onto the plate and I mopped it

up with my finger, making sure I got every last bit. I loved the smell of toast and the taste of jam and margarine on the crunchy bread.

She popped another slice of bread under the grill. In the corner of the kitchen, Ian was in his carrycot. David poured milk on his cornflakes, letting it splash onto the table. Steam rose from the surface of my tea and I blew on it. If I put my hand on the cup it was hot enough to burn. I could only keep it there for a couple of seconds.

The back door was open and sunshine spilled inside. 'Can I go out?' I said.

Mum scraped margarine across my toast and cut it in two, one eye on Ian, who was kicking his legs and making snuffling sounds. She slid the toast onto the plate. 'As long as you don't go far.'

The grass was nearly up to my knees and tickled my bare legs. I had a summer dress on, blue and white gingham with short sleeves and buttons down the front, and I'd wrapped my cardigan round my waist and tied the sleeves together. Like all my other clothes, they had belonged to someone else first. I ran across the field towards a line of trees, cardigan flapping, sending a bee up into the air from the buttercup it was on. The trees stood tall with gnarled branches and masses of thick green leaves. If you stood right underneath and looked up you couldn't see through the green to the sky. It made me think of my favourite Enid Blyton book, *The Magic Faraway Tree*. If I could only climb to the top of one of those trees I'd be in a different world. The sun beat down and I stopped running and squinted up at the sky which was dotted with a few ragged clouds. Not just clouds, I told myself, but secret lands with witches and potions and spells and plants that grew as tall as houses. I sat down in the shade of one of the trees where the ground was cool and thought about how one day I'd find a way of climbing to the top and seeing for myself what was really up there. I picked some daisies and dug a fingernail into the stalks to make slits, then made a chain I hung round my neck, preening as if it was a precious gold necklace studded with jewels given to me by a handsome prince.

The sun was right overhead as I made my way home, still wearing the daisy chain, a buttercup poking through a buttonhole on the front of my dress, and a small bunch of the yellow flowers in my hand for Mum. Out of nowhere, a dog came bounding towards me. It looked just like Lassie off the television. I loved Lassie and felt a buzz of delight as the dog lolloped up, panting in the heat, tongue hanging out. Maybe she was on a rescue mission! I put my hand out to stroke her and she tried to bite me. I pulled my hand back. The dog was snarling, showing pointy teeth. Maybe it wasn't a she. It definitely wasn't Lassie. I started running and the dog came after me. Suddenly, I wished I hadn't gone so far from home. The dog bounded along, brushing against me, barking, as I ran as fast as I could in a straight line across the field. Home seemed miles away. I stumbled and tears streamed down my face. If I fell over the dog would jump on me and that would be that. No one would find me for hours. Days, probably. The back of my neck was damp. The daisy chain leaped about as if it had a mind of its own. The dog barked, showing its sharp teeth. I ran all the way home, and flung myself inside, slamming the back door, tear-stained and heaving for breath. Mum looked up from the sink.

'Make sure you wash your hands, Angela.'

I doubled up and held my side trying to ease the stitch that had kicked in halfway home. I pointed a shaky hand in the direction of the fields. I was completely out of breath. 'A dog chased me. I had to run away.'

Mum stacked a plate on the draining board. 'Get a tea towel and dry these dishes for me.'

'It was like Lassie – a great big thing, snapping at me. It tried to knock me over.'

'Lassie! You watch too much television. No wonder you get so carried away.'

'I'm not getting carried away!' The tears were hot at the back of my eyes.

'Well, I know I could do with a hand.' She gave me a look. 'And I don't suppose Lassie's going to help set the table.'

I stared at her. I had run for my life, chased all the way by a snapping, snarling dog. It had been touch and go I'd even make it home in one piece. I blinked back tears.

She scooped Ian out of his basket. 'I'll change this one and you can do the table.'

I started getting knives and forks out of the drawer. I could put the buttercups in a cup in the middle. She'd like that. Then I could have another go at telling her about the dog, make her believe me this time. I stood holding the cutlery looking for the flowers, then I remembered I'd let go of them as I ran away from Lassie's evil twin.

5

I had been on at my parents to let me have a pet for ages and finally they caved in.

'Come on,' my dad said one Saturday morning, taking my hand. 'Let's go and see if we can find you a guinea pig. Stop you driving me and your poor mum round the bend going on about it all the time.'

It wasn't often I went out with Dad. We'd been to the pictures a couple of times at the ABC on Grimsby Road, to see *Pinocchio* and *Cinderella* as a special treat, Dad all dressed up in a dark suit with a white shirt and navy tie. The foyer of the cinema had been packed with people and Dad kept hold of me while we queued for sweets. The sweets you got at the pictures weren't like the ones you got in other shops. They sold wine gums in big bags and chocolate-covered peanuts in small cardboard boxes. That's what Dad bought, then gave the box to me. I'd shaken it and the peanuts had rattled about inside.

We went to the pet shop in Pasture Street, round the corner from our old house, and I crouched down in front of a cage with guinea pigs. They bustled about, bumping into each other, pushing their noses against the wire, whiskers twitching, letting me put my fingers through the bars to stroke their silky coats. They watched me with their bright little eyes as I breathed in the sawdust smell of the pet shop. Right at the back, past sacks of animal feed and a display of dog leads and matching collars in stiff tan leather was a pen with puppies making yelping sounds. I decided not to get too close. A puppy would be nice but it had been hard enough getting Dad to say yes to a guinea pig, so I wasn't about to push my luck. Behind me, he was giving the man who ran the pet shop a right grilling.

'What are they like to look after? How big do they get? What about the food? I don't want something that's going to eat me out of house and home.'

I had already decided which one I wanted. He had a glossy ginger coat and a bold white stripe running down the centre of his face. I put my finger through the cage and scratched the top of his head. 'Who's a lovely boy, then?' His whiskers twitched. I rubbed his chin. 'You're gorgeous,' I whispered. I already knew what I was going to call him. 'Snoopy,' I said, tapping the wire. 'Come on Snoopy.' He pressed his nose against my finger. I loved him already.

My dad appeared behind me. The pet shop owner, a skinny man with thick spectacles and a brown overall on over his clothes, trailed a couple of steps behind. Dad said, 'Right, have you picked one?'

I pointed at Snoopy. 'Him.'

He peered into the cage. 'What about the white one?'

I shook my head. 'This one's my favourite.' On cue, Snoopy stood on his hind legs and sniffed the air.

'They make wonderful pets,' the pet shop man said, craning to see past my dad.

'It needs to be a boy,' Dad said.

The pet shop man took a hanky from the pocket of his overall and gave his glasses a rub. 'They're all males,' he said, examining his specs. 'That's all we've got at the moment. Just as well you're not looking to breed.'

My Dad made a spluttering sound. 'Breed! It's as much as we can do to look after one!' He gave me a stern look. 'Have you seen the cost of the food? You'll have to do your bit, you know, clean it out and all that. I'm not having your mother do everything.'

'I will; it's my pet.'

'I'll remind you about that when you're trying to get out of cleaning the cage.'

I adored Snoopy. In the afternoons, as soon as I got in from school I'd go to see him. I'd scoop him out of the cage and cuddle him and ask if he'd had a good day while he gazed at me with his solemn little face. He was such a handsome little thing with his distinctive stripe and glossy ginger coat.

Much as I loved him, despite what I'd said to my dad about doing my share of the looking after, it tended to be Mum who cleaned out the cage and kept the food topped up.

One day, I was sitting on the floor with Snoopy in my lap, when Mum came in from the kitchen. 'He was making a bit of a racket today, scrabbling about,' she said. 'Seemed a bit restless.'

'Were you lonely, then?' I said, playing with his ears.

'I don't know about lonely, he was noisy enough.'

'Maybe he was hungry.'

'I'd fed him and he had plenty of water.' She watched him nestling in my lap. 'You don't want to spoil him, Angela. That's probably why he was carrying on – wants a fuss.'

'Naughty boy,' I said, not meaning it, smoothing down the fur on his back.

The next day when I came in from school Mum was waiting for me. 'I've had fun and games with that guinea pig of yours,' she said.

'Why, what's he done?'

'You'd better go and see.'

I searched her face for clues but she was giving nothing away. I dropped my school bag and ran into the sun room, peering into the cage where Snoopy's bright little eyes looked up at me. I dropped to my knees, relieved. Thank goodness, he was all right. Then I spotted the two little shapes beside him, pushing up against his tummy. Snoopy had babies!

Mum came in behind me. 'I thought it was trying to break out of the cage today,' she said. 'The noise of it!'

She had been peeling potatoes when the sound of banging and crashing made her leave what she was doing and come to investigate. Snoopy was rushing about, agitated, running round in circles, and no amount of coaxing or petting would calm him down. *Her*. Mum returned to her potatoes, listening out for further signs of distress from the guinea pig.

When the crashing about finally subsided she came to investigate and found Snoopy, snuggled in a corner, with her babies.

'I dread to think what your dad's going to say when he gets home,' she said, raising an eyebrow.

'Babies! The thing's had babies!' My dad glared at Snoopy in disgust. 'As if I haven't got enough to worry about without two more mouths to feed.'

'They're only little,' I said, my voice a whisper.

Dad pointed an accusing finger at Snoopy, who sniffed the air, unperturbed.

'They're little *now*,' he said. 'What about when they're fully grown?'

Mum gave me a tiny, reassuring nod. 'We'll manage,' she said.

'It was *meant* to be a boy.' Dad looked ready to burst. 'I *asked*.' He turned to my mum. 'I checked and the pet shop bloke swore blind it was a male. I've a good mind to take it back – the lot of them – get my money back.'

'Dad!' My lip trembled.

'Don't you start. Who pays for the food, eh? Who looks after the thing? Me and your mother, that's who.'

I bit my lip.

'Well, we can't do anything now,' Mum said, her voice soothing. 'Come and have your tea and we'll talk about it later.'

'There's nothing to talk about. They're going back. Wait till I see him!'

Mum's mouth twitched.

'It's not funny!'

She shook her head. 'I know, but when you think about it, Ron . . .'

'He must have seen me coming.'

I gave Mum a pleading look.

'We could always find homes for the babies when they're old enough,' she said.

My Dad snorted. 'Or I could just stick them in a box and take them back.'

I wanted to beg him not to but the look on Mum's face warned me to keep quiet. Sometimes my dad's bark was worse than his bite and Mum knew better than anyone how to handle him. After a day or two, Dad stopped threatening to get rid of Snoopy and the babies and started to see the funny side, saying he'd got a bargain paying for one guinea pig and ending up with three. He even joked about putting one over on the pet shop bloke. One day he came home with another cage and when the babies – one pure white and one ginger – were old enough they moved into their own place, leaving Snoopy in peace.

6

Mum sat at the dressing table in her bedroom taking big squashy rollers out of her hair. She ran a brush through the curls, loosening them to create springy waves that settled round her face and neck. She had lovely thick hair, almost jet black. That was its natural colour, and mine was like hers, nearly as dark and about the same length, not quite touching my shoulders and kept off my face with a stretchy hairband. I twisted a strand round my finger making a corkscrew that unravelled as soon as I let it go. She caught my eye in the mirror, smiled, and the skin at the corner of her eyes crinkled. I had her eyes – everybody said so: brown, like dark chocolate. Sometimes I wished my eyes were violet, like Dad's. Mum wore glasses, fashionable ones shaped like a cat's eyes, with a frame that flicked up at the ends and made her look glamorous, even though she didn't have a scrap of make-up on. She patted her hair and picked up the bottle of Coty L'Aimant on the dressing table, dabbing some at the base of her throat and behind her ears. I held out my hands and she stroked the perfume wand across the inside of my wrists. It made me think of the flower stall in the market and the way the roses smelled if you put your face right up close to the petals.

Mum had on a plain sleeveless dress over a blouse that fastened in a bow at the neck. It was quite a dressy outfit for her but she always looked her best for the meetings at Kingdom Hall. She picked up her gloves and put a fresh white hanky from her top drawer into her handbag, a stiff black boxy one with a silver clasp and a short handle that fitted in the crook of her arm, and snapped it shut. I got up off the edge of the bed and smoothed my skirt the way she did.

When we got to Kingdom Hall one of the women from the congregation came up to Mum. She'd brought a bag of clothes for us. 'There's a few bits that'll do for Angela, one or two dresses, and some shirts and things for the boys,' she said.

I felt a prickle of excitement. I loved it when people brought us stuff – getting back home, going through it all and ending up with loads of new things. New to us, anyway. Everything in the bags was hand-me-downs. The woman, in a bottle-green coat with big buttons and a shawl collar, seemed to tower over Mum, who was tiny compared to most other people, including Dad. He seemed about twice her size to me. One day I'd asked how tall she was and she said she was an inch under five foot and Dad was a six-footer.

I didn't always want to go to the Christian meetings but Mum put her foot down. It was all right for my dad not to go and he never minded Mum being out on Tuesday and Thursday evenings and Sunday mornings. He said he could see how much the meetings helped and she always seemed really happy there, even though I'd get fidgety sitting still for hours on end. I'd heard her say she didn't know what she'd have done after Trevor died if it hadn't been for the Witnesses coming to the door. The people at Kingdom Hall were ever so nice and kind, giving Ian cuddles, patting me and David on the head, saying how pleased they were to see us. You could tell they meant it, the way they were always smiling and making Mum smile, too. I just wished we didn't have to go so often and stay so long when I could have been playing out instead. We'd be sat there for what felt like an age while people went up to the platform at the front to give talks and read passages from the Bible. Mum would have her Bible on her lap, running a finger down the page, following the readings, sometimes going up to the lectern to do a talk. There was always singing and that was the bit I liked best.

At home, Mum undid the knot on the bin bag we'd been given and spread the clothes on the settee. There was a navy pleated skirt for me and a pink cardigan with buttons shaped like flowers. I picked out a grey tunic and a pale blue blouse with short sleeves and a Peter Pan collar. There was a light blue anorak that looked good as new. I put it on and zipped it up, tugging at the sleeves, which were a bit too long. Mum leaned over and folded the cuffs back. The lining was a shade or two darker than the jacket and shiny, like satin. I put my hands in the pockets, liking the slippery feel of the fabric, and did a twirl. Mum smiled. 'That looks lovely, Angela. Don't forget to say thank you to your Aunty Eileen the next time you see her.'

I had lots of new aunties now through being in what we called 'the truth'. In the summer holidays we'd gone to Yorkshire to see Aunty Vera and one day we got a coach with lots of other Witnesses to an assembly at Hillsborough Football Ground in Sheffield. Aunty Vera lived a few miles away in Barnsley. The stadium had been filled with thousands of people from all over the country and it was just like the meetings we went to at home with people at the front doing talks and reading Scripture. The only difference was being outside in such a big crowd. Aunty Vera had a son, Philip, who was nine, the same age as me. She let us eat homemade chocolate cake in the cupboard under the stairs, which we'd made into a den.

Mum sorted through the rest of the clothes, making a pile of shorts and shirts for the boys. There was a jumper, a maroon slipover with a V-neck and a cable design at the front, that would do for David and, once he grew out of it, Ian. We never had brand new things but it didn't matter because we always had plenty of clothes that were new to us and Mum would let me choose things from the second-hand shops when she could afford it. The Austrian-style pinafore with the puff-sleeved blouse I'd found in a shop in Pasture Street was my favourite. I'd even worn it when I had my school photo done.

Mum smiled as she folded everything up ready to put away. I knew it was a struggle making ends meet and that what Dad gave her from his wage packet on a Friday night had to last all week. It didn't always stretch and sometimes she'd come up with some fancy-sounding meal for tea that would turn out to be nothing more than potatoes with a bit of gravy because the housekeeping had run out and that was all that was left in the larder.

I could see why she liked being a Witness and how

much everybody there helped out. Whenever I tried to get out of going to meetings she'd say it would do me the world of good. According to her, the people at Kingdom Hall were family.

7

I was round at my best friend Wendy Bradley's house, in the kitchen, cutting up crumbly cheese for sandwiches. It was 1972, 'Puppy Love' had got to Number One, and we were both mad about Donny Osmond. I had cut his picture out of *Jackie* and made it into a cover for my spelling book. The cheese fell apart as I cut into it. White cheese sandwiches were our favourite. Wendy was at the cooker, pouring soup from a tin into a pan.

'You've got to try this,' she said, taking a wooden spoon from a holder on the kitchen counter and giving the liquid a stir. 'It's fab.'

I had never tasted Heinz tomato soup before.

Wendy lived in a big posh house on Yarborough Road. The kitchen had all sorts of stuff I wasn't used to. In the drawer with all the knives and forks I spotted a proper potato peeler with bright orange cord coiled round the handle. At home, we used a knife to peel potatoes. Wendy's place was always neat and tidy, unlike ours which was a bit of a tip. My baby sister, Rebecca – Becky – had come along by then and Mum fought a losing battle to get us all to tidy up. There was stuff everywhere. It drove her mad.

Mum never went out to work after Trevor died. She stayed at home and looked after us. She always had her hands full and was forever in the kitchen peeling great piles of potatoes, cooking, cleaning, or doing endless loads of laundry in the old twin tub washer. The ironing basket was always full. I helped out, peeling veg and washing-up.

'I'm having a dishwasher when I grow up,' I'd say, making her laugh.

Wendy tucked her blonde hair behind her ears and turned the heat down under the soup as it started to bubble. She had a round, pretty face and she wore lovely clothes. I had my best dress on, the one I'd found in the shop on Pasture Street. As soon as I saw it I had wanted it. It was perfect with its crisp white puff sleeves and pinafore front embroidered in blue and pink. It made me think of something from *The Sound of Music*. I had held it up against me and begged Mum to let me have it. It wasn't cheap, five shillings – twenty-five pence in new money – but she could see how much I wanted it and most of the time I didn't get a say in what clothes I got. I wore that dress all the time. I knew most of my clothes weren't as nice as Wendy's but she never said anything.

I cut the sandwiches in half. 'My mum was going to get Heinz spaghetti,' I said, 'but Dad wouldn't have it. He said it's foreign.'

Wendy pulled a face. 'We have that. You put it on toast and it's really nice. You butter the toast and the sauce makes the bread all soggy.'

She tipped the soup into bowls that were like big cups with handles and a picture of a steaming bowl of soup on the side. I dipped my spoon in and blew on the piping hot liquid. Just as she'd said, it tasted amazing, creamy, rich and sweet. We never had food like that at home.

Wendy put her spoon down and had a bite of her sandwich. 'I'm never going to eat cheese unless it's the crumbly kind,' she said. 'I hate the orange rubbery stuff.'

I couldn't help thinking how lucky she was, having all the crumbly cheese she could eat and Heinz tomato soup whenever she wanted it.

She looked at me over her bowl. The soup had stained her mouth bright red. Mine was probably the same.

Wendy said, 'Do you really not keep Christmas?'

I shook my head. 'We don't believe in it. It's because we're Witnesses.'

'What about presents?'

'We don't have presents.'

'Not even from your mum and dad?'

I gave a shrug. 'My nana sneaks us a chocolate off the tree, a snowman or something, when we go round there the day after Boxing Day.'

Wendy stared at me. Her cheeks were flushed from the piping-hot soup. 'You don't have a tree?'

'No. We don't do anything special.'

'You must do *some*thing. Put up decorations anyway.'

'We don't. Mum says it's just another day.' Wendy was silent. I said, 'We watch telly.'

'What about your Christmas dinner?'

'We just have what we'd have anyway – egg and chips or something. My dad makes great chips.'

Not long before it had been Wendy's birthday and she'd had a party at home for all her friends from school. I couldn't go because we didn't celebrate birthdays, not that I really understood why. Wendy had got loads of cards and nice things. On my birthday, on 28 April, she'd sneaked me a card that ended up hidden at the bottom of my schoolbag. It was the only card I got.

In our house, it would be your birthday and nobody would say a thing. There'd be no special breakfast, no card, nothing. I'd got into a bit of a row with Mum about no one making a fuss when any of us had our birthdays. She said it was because we were Witnesses and went on about the Bible and Herod's birthday and John the Baptist's head ending up on a plate. I couldn't see what that had to do with anything.

'It's not like you don't know when my birthday is but I never even get a card,' I said.

'That's enough, Angela.'

'Everyone else has parties and cake and all sorts.'

'We're not everyone else.'

I didn't tell her that being a Witness made me the odd one out at school and that I wanted to be like the other girls and go to birthday parties, maybe even have one of my own. I was awkward and shy, never putting my hand up in class, going red if a teacher singled me out for something. More than anything, I was desperate to blend into the background, but our faith meant I was always going to stand out.

8

The police were at the door, two officers in uniform, asking for Dad. They came in and sat in the front room, making the place feel small. Mum sent us out, but the door was open and I stood in the hall listening.

They'd come about Dad's brother, our Uncle Arthur. One of the policemen said it was bad news and he was very sorry. I couldn't hear everything he said. Something about a car crossing onto the wrong side of the road and hitting Uncle Arthur's head-on. My aunty Ellen was in the passenger seat with the two kids in the back. They were all right but Uncle Arthur was dead. They'd been going on their holidays – I'd heard Mum and Dad talking about it.

The policemen said something about seeing themselves out. I stared at my feet as they went past, down the hall and out the front door, pulling it to so it didn't bang. Back in the living room Dad had his head in his hands. His face was wet. Mum sat on the edge of the armchair with her arm round him, tears running down her cheeks.

9

I must have been about eleven when we moved to Brere-ton Avenue in Cleethorpes, to a house with enormous bay windows that faced onto the park. I could tell it was a posh area because the girl next door was called Margot and her dad was a captain on a big ship. They even had a white poodle, a proper pedigree with a fancy hair cut and ever such a cute la-de-da way of carrying on.

With four children to look after, Mum was busier than ever, always up to her eyes with housework. The bigger house meant there was even more to do in the way of cleaning and tidying, not that she ever really managed to keep on top of things. Thanks to us lot leaving a trail of destruction wherever we went the place was always a mess.

'Let's think about what we can have for dinner this week,' she said one day as she heaved sodden sheets from the washer into the spin dryer, doing her best not to slop water onto the kitchen floor. There had to be an easier way to do the laundry. She dried her hands and took a list out of the pocket of her housecoat.

I was at the sink peeling potatoes. I dumped the peelings in the bin and the pair of us pored over the shopping list.

'If I get a bit of stewing beef we could get two or three meals out of it. Have it with mash one night,' she said.

'You could do it in the oven and put sliced potato on top,' I chipped in.

Mum made a note. 'I'll think of something for another night as well.'

Whatever she came up with, one thing was certain – it would involve a good helping of spuds. We had potatoes with everything.

'I'll do us liver and onions on Thursday,' she said.

My heart sank. I hated liver and onions.

'With a bit of mash,' Mum said. 'That should do it. Then your dad can do his Clement Freud bit on Friday.'

Once a week Dad took over in the kitchen and made a big pan of chips for tea. That was his treat.

Raised voices came from the hall. Mum gave me a weary look. In the corner, the twin tub jerked and gave a high-pitched squeal as the spin dryer picked up speed. She slid her paper with its meals all planned out back inside her pocket and said, 'Just go and see what those boys are up to now, Angela.'

In the hall, Ian hovered at the foot of the stairs bawling his eyes out. Upstairs on the landing, a gleeful David taunted him, 'Cry baby, cry baby.'

Ian opened his mouth and let out a wail.

David had looped a tie round the neck of his little brother's favourite teddy and was now dangling it over the banister at the top of the stairs.

Ian gazed up at him, tears running down his face. 'Let him *go*!'

'Let him go? What – you mean like this?' David pretended to drop the tie and the teddy, head lolling, body swinging from side to side, dropped a few inches.

43

Ian's face contorted. 'MUM!'

I went to give him a cuddle but he shook me off. 'Come on now – shush,' I said. I turned to David. 'Leave him alone.'

David jerked the teddy about on the tie. 'What you going to do about it?'

'Just put his teddy back where you found it, will you?'

At seven years old, Ian was already a neat child who insisted on order. He wasn't the type to leave his toys lying about or – heaven forbid – chuck them into a toy box. Everything he owned, from his collection of metal cars to the beloved teddies, had its place. At the foot of the bed, the teddies sat shoulder to shoulder, always in the same order. He absolutely adored them and one thing guaranteed to send him off the deep end was David mucking about with his stuff. It caused endless rows which David, two years older, almost always started.

I began to head up the stairs.

'Ooh, I can't hold him!' David grinned and leaned further over the banister, lowering the teddy. Ian covered his eyes. His hands were clenched in tight fists.

'MUM!'

Mum's voice reached us from the kitchen. 'Just be*have* yourselves. If I have to come out there, there'll be trouble.'

I pictured her, hair damp from the steam rising off the pan of potatoes now boiling on the stove, a pile of washing waiting to be hung out. She never stopped.

'Give it here,' I told David, marching up the stairs.

'Oops.'

The teddy fell to the floor, landing face down next to Ian, who sank to his knees and cradled his toy in his arms.

I glared at David. He grinned back, delighted. 'Do you have to be so mean?' I snapped before racing back down the stairs.

I knelt beside my little brother, who had his teddy, still sporting one of my dad's ties, pressed tight to his chest. 'Let's take him upstairs,' I said.

Ian said nothing. He was sobbing, a soft hiccupping sound.

'He might want a lie down.'

Ian's voice was small. 'He's got a bad head.'

'We'll put him to bed, then, let him have a little sleep.' I took his hand and led him into the living room where we made a bed on the settee out of cushions and one of my doll's blankets. Ian tucked his teddy in. A pair of big brown eyes gazed up at him. David clattered down the stairs and came to stand in the doorway.

'Cry baby,' he said under his breath.

Mum bustled about in the kitchen, lifting the lid on a pan with liver simmering in an onion and gravy sauce, and giving it a stir. Ian and David hung about, getting under her feet. She ruffled their hair as she went in and out setting the table, ready for my dad to come in from his shift at the docks where he worked pulling in the boats. In the seventies, Grimsby was one of the biggest and busiest fishing ports in the country and the docks were one of the main employers in the town.

'No winding your dad up,' Mum said, bending and planting a kiss on Ian's head. We always knew as soon as the door opened and my dad appeared what kind of mood he was in – it would be written all over his face. Mum tucked David's shirt into the back of his trousers, giving him a cuddle at the same time. 'Look at the state of you, Sloppy Joe.' She sounded playful. David's socks were round his ankles and she bent and tugged at them. 'Let's smarten you up a bit, like your brother.'

Ian was immaculate as usual: face scrubbed clean, socks pulled up to the knee, hair short and sharp, nothing out of place. Mum gave him a hug. 'You smell of Palmolive,' she said, pleased.

I worked my way through the pile of ironing in the basket while she drained the potatoes, added margarine and mashed them with a fork, leaving them in the pan on the stove with the lid on. The gas was turned right down under the liver.

'Your dad's going to be in any minute,' she said, taking a plate of sliced white bread and marge into the other room.

I was about halfway through the ironing when the front door opened and a minute or two later Dad in his work jeans and a thick jumper came into the kitchen. The room seemed to shrink. I gave him a hopeful look but he was frowning and rubbing his hands together.

'Bitter out there today,' he said, glowering at the boys, as if having to work outside in the cold was their fault.

Mum was already pouring him a cup of tea. 'This'll warm you up.' Her voice was soothing. 'Tea's ready.'

'I'm starving.'

He took his tea and went. I glanced at Mum. We both knew from the look on his face that he had come home in a bad mood.

At the table we ate in silence, knives and forks scraping on the plates. I swallowed down the liver.

Dad gave David a sharp look. 'Stop playing with your food.'

David kept his head down and dragged a tiny morsel of liver through the gravy on his plate.

'Get it down you – cutting it up like a baby.'

David pushed the food round his plate, tracing patterns in the gravy. Dad put his fork down and held his knife upright, the heel resting on the table, his attention now on Ian. Mum had cut his food up for him. He was taking his time getting through it and was busy turning his mashed potato into a perfect little mound.

47

'Give me strength,' Dad said, livid. His eyes darted from Ian to David and back to Ian. 'Look at the pair of you – like a couple of girls.' His knife clattered onto his plate and flecks of gravy landed on the cloth, a checked one that was clean on that night.

Mum said, 'Leave them be, they're not doing any harm.'

'They're a pair of cissies!'

I kept eating, working my way through what was left of the liver on my plate. I smothered it in mash and swallowed.

Ian had stopped eating. David aimed a kick at him under the table and his face started to crumple. 'Mum . . .'

Dad's expression darkened. 'Oh, for crying out loud, here we go. Run to your mother. Can't I just have my tea in peace?'

Ian shot a pleading look at Mum. David sniggered. Dad turned on him. 'And what do you think you're laughing at?' David shrank in his seat. 'I'll give you a good hiding, the pair of you.'

Mum put down her knife and fork. 'Ron, can we not just finish our meal?'

'They need toughening up,' he said, still glaring at the boys. 'You've got them soft.' He pushed back his chair. 'You two, come with me.'

Ian and David stayed put as Dad undid his belt and yanked it out of the loops of his jeans. He slapped the belt against the palm of his hand. 'If you think I'm coming in after a day slogging on the docks to put up with cheek from you two you can think again.'

'Ron . . .'

'Get on your feet.' His voice was a bark '*Now!*'

David flinched and scrambled off his chair. Ian gave Mum one last desperate look before Dad grabbed him by the arm and lifted him onto his feet. He strode out of the room, both boys dragging along behind him.

Mum closed her eyes.

From the room next door came the sound of David crying and Ian bawling, already in a state about what was to come. 'No, no, no. I didn't *do* anything,' Ian whimpered. I pictured the two of them facing the wall, having to bend over and wait for the beating. I'd had plenty of hidings and there was nothing 'good' about them. You could hardly sit down afterwards. Dad's furious voice drowned Ian out. 'Don't answer me back,' he bellowed. The belt came down. 'Learn to do as you're told . . . you'll not cheek me . . . pair of girls.'

I helped Mum clear the table.

Our home economics teacher at Yarborough Road Junior School had long hair pinned up at the sides with tortoise-shell clips that matched her glasses. She had pale skin and a wide mouth.

I sat next to Wendy, writing 'I love Donny' in the back of my book when the teacher wasn't looking. Wendy flipped her book open to the back page. 'I love Donny' was written over and over with a little heart and an arrow through it.

The lesson was about personal hygiene.

'I'm going to talk about washing your hair, keeping it clean and healthy,' the teacher said. 'When you wash your hair, girls, always use warm, not hot water. Hot water can make it greasy. And always rinse out all the shampoo.' She gazed round the room. Her own hair was a gleaming red curtain that bounced when she moved. She was writing *warm water* on the board. I wasn't sure if we were sup-posed to copy it down so I put the date at the top of a new page, just to look busy.

Wendy did the same.

'Does anyone wash their hair in the bath?'

I put my hand up.

The teacher's eyes narrowed. 'Angela Chapman, I hope you don't just dunk your hair in the dirty bath water.'

'Yes, Miss.'

'In the same water you *bathe* in?'

'Yes, Miss.'

Someone sniggered and a girl with neat, jaw-length, poker-straight blonde hair pulled a face and pinched her nose. 'Isn't that dirty, Miss?'

Miss nodded. 'Yes, it is.'

I didn't like to say I also had to share the bathwater with my brothers and sister. Water in our house was precious. Hot water cost money. The immersion heater went on long enough to heat up what we needed then it went straight off. I had never thought twice about us all sharing the same water. I thought it was normal. I didn't see what was wrong with washing my hair in the bath either.

'One of those shower attachments on the taps, Angela, for your hair. That's what you should be doing.'

I nodded. 'Yes, Miss.' I didn't like the sound of a shower attachment. By the time the bath was full there was no hot water left in the tank and I didn't fancy washing my hair in cold water. Mum said that's what gave you a chill.

When the bell went at the end of the day I was still thinking about the home economics lesson.

I said to Wendy, 'Is it dirty washing my hair like that?'

She linked arms. 'Don't be daft, I do it as well. I just wasn't going to tell *her*.'

We were going round to Wendy's house. I don't know why, but we decided to take a short cut the back way past the empty milk crates stacked up ready to be collected the next morning. What we called the 'milk doors' were strictly out of bounds but as long as no one caught us it was no big deal. The corridor was empty and we sneaked out, giggling. Next thing we knew, there was the sound of breaking glass. I'd kicked over a stray bottle and smashed it. We froze and I stared at Wendy as the door swung open and one of the prefects, a hefty girl with lank hair and a mouth that turned down at the corners, took a step towards us.

'What are you doing out here?'

'I . . . we're . . . I mean, we're going home,' I stuttered, feeling the heat rise in my face.

'You're not allowed to use this door.'

I gave her an apologetic look.

'You'll need to see the headmistress.'

She marched us back inside, down the corridor to the Head's office, and tapped on the door. 'Wait here,' she told us as the Headmistress's voice boomed out. 'Come in!'

My heart thumped in my chest. I had never been sent to the Head. I glanced at Wendy and saw the panic in her eyes. Inside the Head's office I could see the prefect's lank hair, her head bobbing about as she dropped us in it. After a minute or two she came out.

'You can go in now, the pair of you,' she said, giving us a frosty look.

I went in first. I couldn't remember whose idea it was to sneak through the milk doors but it was me who'd got us caught, knocking over that bottle. That's what brought Miss Perfect, the prefect, running. My legs felt peculiar.

The Head looked at us stony-faced across the desk. She adjusted the narrow spectacles on her nose and pursed her lips.

'How long have you been at this school?'

Neither of us spoke. I glanced at Wendy. She looked ready to cry. I blinked hard.

'Long enough to know you do not leave by the milk doors. Never. No matter what.' She gave us a long, hard look. 'I'm sure we would all like to be the first to leave when the bell goes. I certainly have better things to do with my time than stay behind dealing with girls who can't do as they're told.' She glared at me and then at Wendy.

She got to her feet and went to the cabinet in the corner behind her desk. Her grey skirt had sharp creases up the back from where she'd been sitting on it. 'We have rules for a reason. You may think I dream them up for the fun of it but I can assure you I do not.' She opened the cabinet and stared at the contents for a moment. When she turned to face us she was holding a slipper.

'Pull up your skirt.'

I did as I was told and she landed half a dozen blows on the top of my leg. I winced as I let go of my skirt. My leg throbbed. Wendy was next.

'I don't want to see either of you girls again,' she said, shutting the slipper away in the cabinet. 'Off you go.'

12

Mum was busy in the kitchen as usual and I'd said I'd get on with the ironing. David and Ian were playing in the other room. Rebecca was in there too. The house was peaceful, too peaceful. There was a loud thump and my mum looked up from the sink where she was scrubbing at a pan.

I ran the iron along one of my mum's blouses.

From the other room came a sudden thud and shouting. Mum stiffened. I said, 'I'll go and tell them to cut it out.' David and Ian could hardly spend five minutes together without fighting.

David was in the centre of the room with one of Ian's toys, a bright red sports car with doors and a bonnet that opened, held high above his head. Ian was jumping up, pulling at David's jumper, trying to get the car back.

'Give it back,' I said.

David twisted away from Ian and lobbed the car over the back of the settee. 'Go and get it, baby,' he mocked.

Ian pushed past him and dived over the sofa.

I started to say, 'I wish you'd not wind him up—' just as Ian's head bobbed up over the back of the sofa and he hurled the car at David. It bounced off his shoulder.

'Ow, that—'

Ian came round the sofa picking up more toys, turning them into missiles, flinging them across the room. David retreated into the next room, where my little sister, Rebecca, was on the floor, playing. David's shape could be seen through the glass partition. Ian flung the toy in his hand at the wall. He was screaming and working himself into a frenzy.

I said, 'Ian . . .' but he turned his back and rummaged through the toys lying around. I saw him eye the pool table. Then he yanked a dart from the board, turned and aimed it at the shape on the other side of the glass. The dart shattered the partition and flew past Becky's head. There was a moment of silence.

I shouted for Mum. 'You'd better come!'

In the other room, David stood stock still, broken glass all over the floor, Becky beside him, the dart in the middle of the debris. He put a hand to his head and blurted out, 'He nearly killed me!'

Ian's wailing had reached full volume and he was hurling anything he could get his hands on. Toys bounced off the walls. One of the pool cues went flying. Mum did her best to hold onto him and calm him down but he wasn't having it. His screams got louder and more frantic until, in despair, she sent for my dad.

The door flew open and Dad burst into the room. Being dragged away from work to sort out a naughty boy had sent his stress levels soaring long before he got anywhere near home.

'What on *earth* is going on?' he asked, taking in the wreckage, the smashed glass. Ian chucked a tractor at him. It hit him square in the chest. Dad's face darkened. 'You little . . .' He turned to Mum. 'You – you let him get away with murder. He needs a good hiding, that'll stop all this nonsense once and for all.' He started to take his belt off while Ian flailed about and kicked at the toys littering the floor. None of us had seen him like this before. Dad stopped in his tracks, belt at the ready.

'Right,' he told Ian. 'So that's how you behave. We scrimp and save so you can have all this' – he gestured at the toys littering the place – 'and you – you just want to smash them up.' He took a step closer to Ian, towering over him. 'You think money grows on trees?' Ian's screams got louder. He kicked out at my dad.

'Please yourself,' Dad said, wheeling round and striding out of the room. In the kitchen he flung open a cupboard door, tore a couple of bin liners off a roll, and ran up the stairs to Ian's room, grabbing the teddies lined up on the bed, stuffing them into one of the plastic sacks. He went around the room scooping up every toy Ian possessed, until both bags were full.

Downstairs, he held up his spoils triumphantly. Ian was still bawling. 'Think you can carry on like that and get away with it?' he said. 'You've got too much, that's what's wrong. Spoiled, the lot of you. Learn to do as you're told.'

Dad turned to Mum. 'I have to get back to work.' He hoisted a bag over his shoulder. 'This lot's going to the tip.'

13

Dad was in one of his good moods. He came home from work, went straight to the living room and put an Elvis Presley record on the radiogram, volume cranked up loud. He dragged Mum out of the kitchen and the pair of them danced to 'Return to Sender', Dad singing along, Mum making a half-hearted attempt to protest.

'Leave off, you daft thing,' she said, chuckling, as he tipped her so far back her hair almost grazed the carpet.

'No such number,' Dad crooned in her ear, rocking her back and forth. 'No such phone.' He grinned and his eyes shone. 'I was a Teddy Boy, you know, when I met your mum. Better looking than Elvis, I was. Swept her off her feet.' He gave her a wink.

Mum gave him a playful shove. 'Will you listen to him?'

They were good dancers. Every year on the first of March, their wedding anniversary, they'd throw a little party and have a bop. It was the only time anyone in our house bought presents.

I said, 'Play "Teddy Bear".' That was my favourite. I knew nearly all the words and the bits I didn't I made up.

Whenever Elvis went on it meant we didn't have to keep out of my dad's way and tiptoe about the place. Walking on eggshells, Mum called it. We could all join in and have a dance.

'Go on, have a mad half hour,' Dad said, doing some

kind of fancy jive, showing off, lifting my mum off her feet.

The Miss World competition was a big deal in our house. We always lined up in front of the TV to watch it. I loved the costumes, the glamorous girls, the amazing prizes. If a girl won Miss World she got to visit loads of different countries and go out with famous men. It all seemed a million miles away from life in Grimsby.

In 1974 Helen Morgan was Miss UK. I thought she was beautiful but it was impossible to pick the girl who'd take the crown because, to be honest, they all looked lovely to me.

'They'll go for a brunette this year,' Dad said. 'Bound to.'

The year before it was blonde Miss USA Marjorie Wallace who had won. She was all over the papers, pictured having fun with the likes of George Best and Tom Jones. The Miss World people can't have been impressed by this because she didn't keep the title for long.

I wondered where all these girls came from and how the whole beauty pageant business worked. They must be special to start with. Yet according to the commentary, Helen Morgan came from a little town in Wales and worked in a bank. That didn't sound so unusual to me. How had she gone from working in a bank to being in the final of Miss World?

'She might win, you know, Miss UK,' Dad said, when they were down to the last few girls and Eric Morley in his dinner suit, hair slicked back, announced that the votes had been cast and he had the envelope with the results.

There was a drum roll. Helen Morgan was one of just six girls left in the running. 'Second runner-up,' Eric Morley said. The drum roll reached a crescendo. 'Miss Israel.'

'First runner-up . . . Miss South Africa.'

'And Miss World, 1974, is . . .'

'She's got it,' Dad said, sitting forward in his chair.

'Miss UK, Helen Morgan.'

I watched this lovely leggy girl with her shiny hair and fabulous smile, not so long ago a bank worker from Barry in Wales, blink back tears as the winner's anthem played and she made her way the length of the catwalk, a crown on her head, a sash proclaiming her the most beautiful girl in the world. Flashbulbs popped as dozens of photographers snapped away. She looked radiant.

'Told you,' Dad said, pleased.

The credits had just started to roll when a strange scuffling sound came from the chimney. I looked at Dad. There it was again, definitely something scratching. Before we could move, a small ball of fur fell from the chimney into the hearth.

Dad jumped up. 'What the . . . ?'

It was a rodent, grey and filthy.

Dad peered at it. 'It's a bloody rat!'

I got up. 'No, hang on, I think it's . . .' I moved closer. The creature was on its back legs, whiskers twitching, sniffing the air. 'It's . . . Snowy!'

A few weeks earlier we'd got a hamster and someone had left the door of the cage open. Snowy had done a runner. We had turned the place upside looking for him.

I picked up the bedraggled little soul in the fireplace. You'd never have guessed he was meant to be white.

Dad was scratching his head. 'Where's the little so and so been all this time? Mo, look who's here.'

Mum came in and peered at Snowy. 'Are you sure that's him? Look at the colour of him.'

'He just needs a bath.'

Dad shook with laughter. 'Never mind Snowy, more like Houdini! How did he get up the chimney?'

Mum said, 'He doesn't look like he's starving, anyway. What's he been eating all this time?'

I put Snowy back in his cage and made sure the door was firmly shut. The next day I gave him a bath and made him white again, just in case anyone thought the hamster who'd fallen down the chimney was an impostor.

A few days after the Miss World competition had been on TV, Dad came in from work and announced that Helen Morgan had lost her title. 'She's got a little lad,' he said, 'so she's given back the crown.'

It didn't matter to me. Never mind what anyone said, she had gone out there and beaten everybody else fair and square to win Miss World. A girl from a place called Barry somewhere in Wales. It made you think.

14

I shared a bedroom with David, Ian and Rebecca. The boys had bunks against one wall and a double bed was pushed against the opposite wall. There wasn't much space in between. On rainy days when we were stuck indoors I'd sometimes sit them down and read stories from *The Magic Faraway Tree*. Ever since I'd found the book on a stall in the market in Grimsby I couldn't put it down. The stories of three children who move house and find an enchanted wood on their doorstep had all of us captivated. We loved to imagine it was us climbing the tree into another world, going on adventures to fantastic places like the land of Take-What-You-Want where you could have as much of anything and it didn't cost a penny, or the Land of Spells filled with wizards and green-eyed witches.

I said, 'I know, let's do a magic spell and go to another land.'

Ian clapped his hands. 'The Land of Toys!'

David gave him a thump on the shoulder. 'The Lost Island!'

I folded my arms. 'What about if we just climb the tree and see where we end up?'

I started climbing the ladder to the top bunk, making a meal of it, pretending I was clambering from one branch to the next. Ian and David scurried up after me. We sat cross-legged on the bunk. I swayed back and forth and put out my hands for balance. 'Ooh, I think we're in the Rocking Land,' I said, grinning.

Ian clutched the bedspread. 'It's moving!'

David rolled his eyes but his fingers curled around the headboard. 'It's a boat! I can see land.'

We all leaned forward and peered at my bed below. I had just read the story of the little lost island where a gust of wind had carried everyone through the air and dropped them onto a sandy beach. So it was probably my idea to jump from the top bunk onto the bed below. It felt wild and reckless as I leapt off and landed on the mattress. David was next, landing beside me with a thud. Ian knelt on the edge of the bunk. I held out my arms. 'Come on, just pretend you're flying!' He flung himself at me and the three of us flopped in a heap on the bed, in stitches.

David was first back on his feet and up the ladder. 'Let's do it again!'

Ian shot up behind him and I followed. One by one we sailed through the air, my bed softening our landing. All thought of the lost island vanished. The game became jumping off the top bunk onto the bed below. We did it over and over until I landed for the umpteenth time and there was a horrible snapping sound as the bed collapsed. I stared up at my brothers. David's eyes were wide. Ian had his hands over his mouth.

Mum's voice came up the stairs. 'What on earth's going on up there? You sound like you're coming through the ceiling!'

We shot each other frantic looks, David and Ian trying

to look as though whatever had just happened was nothing to do with them. David lay on his stomach and snatched up a model of a fire engine, fiddling with the turntable ladder. Ian sat with his back to the wall, hugging a pillow. I knelt on the bed facing the door. Mum flew in, her face furious, a duster in her hand. She took one look at the bed tipped up at one end.

'What have you done?' She was looking at me, waiting for an answer. Before I could say anything, she bent, lifted the bedspread and retrieved a splintered bit of wood. 'You've broken it – it's in bits,' she said, appalled.

I glanced up at the bunk. David kept his back to me and Ian hugged the pillow harder.

Mum rounded on me. 'What were you doing?'

I shook my head. 'Just . . . just playing.'

'*Playing!* I'm surprised you didn't end up in the room below.' She gazed at the bed, like a boat that had capsized and not quite managed to come all the way back to the surface. I had hold of the bedspread, as if I really was in Rocking Land and could slide off if I let go. 'You, Angela,' Mum was saying, 'you should know better.'

I wondered if there was any way we could put things right before Dad got home. As if she could see inside my head, she said, 'Wait until your dad gets home.' I felt a knot of panic in my stomach.

'Maybe we can fix it!' I sounded desperate.

'I don't think so.' She held up the ruined leg. 'Look at the state of it. There's no fixing it. How did you manage to make such a mess?'

I stared at the buttons on my cardigan. 'We were only jumping.'

Mum gasped. I sneaked a look at her. She was gazing at the top bunk where Ian and David were doing their best to keep out of things. 'Don't tell me you've been jumping from up there.' She turned back to me. 'You could have killed yourselves. Have you no sense?'

Dad was livid. He sounded like an echo of my mum. 'You're the eldest, Angela, you're supposed to have more sense.' He glared at David and Ian. 'And what do you think you two were playing at?'

David stared at his shoes. 'Angela said we could.'

Dad bent down so their faces were almost touching. 'And if Angela told you to jump off a cliff would you do it?' He straightened up and shook his head. 'I'm sick of this. I come home from work and all I want is a bit of peace. And where's the money coming from for a new bed? ' He undid his belt and yanked it out of the loops. 'You're all getting a good hiding.'

Ian shot me a terrified look. I took a deep breath and said, 'It was my fault.'

Dad shook the belt at me. 'I'm not daft. I worked that out already.'

'You don't need to hit them two.'

He gave me an ugly smile. 'So you're telling me what I can and can't do in my own house now?'

'No, I . . .'

'All three of you turn round and face the wall.'

He made us bend down, one after the other. I went first, the belt whacking me across the behind over and over, the pain making me cry. David was next, then Ian, in tears long before it was his turn. He was the smallest and

I just hoped by the time Dad got to him he wouldn't be so angry any more.

'Right, bed – and I don't want to hear another sound out of any of you tonight.'

Mum came out of the kitchen as I was on my way up the stairs. 'Oh no, you don't,' she said. 'Come back down here. I want a word with you.'

I trailed behind her into the living room. Dad looked up from the *Grimsby Evening Telegraph*. 'Where've you been?'

'School.'

'Until this time?'

'I was with some mates.'

Dad snorted. 'We know all about your so-called mates.'

Mum said, 'We know you're seeing a lad.'

Someone must have seen me and Mark, my boyfriend, and told on us. I gave her a defiant look. 'So what?'

Dad put his paper down. 'So what? You don't go seeing lads behind our back.'

Mum pursed her lips. 'That lad, he's not in *the truth*, Angela. He's not a Witness.'

I rolled my eyes. I had been seeing Mark for a couple of weeks and I was mad about him. He was the new boy at school, fifteen, a couple of years older than me, and the minute I'd clapped eyes on him I fancied him. He was good-looking in a swarthy, rocker kind of way, with long hair and big brown eyes and the kind of smile that made my stomach do funny little flips. Chelsea was his team and he came to school with a blue and white scarf knotted round his neck and a denim jacket with the club's name emblazoned on the back. He was the coolest boy I'd ever seen and it was me he wanted to go out with.

Mum was saying, 'You're only thirteen. It's too young to be seeing lads.'

'I'm not seeing *lads* – his name's Mark.'

Dad's brow was a mass of frown lines. 'I don't care if he's Prince flaming Charming – you're not seeing him.'

I stomped off upstairs and slammed my bedroom door.

Mark was calling round for me. I put on a black stretchy top and a pair of drainpipe trousers and applied thick black liner to my eyes. I made my lashes look huge, loading on the mascara. We'd only be going to sit on the swings in the park over the road or something but I wanted to look my best. When the doorbell went I grabbed my jacket and was halfway down the stairs when Dad opened the door.

Mark stood on the bottom step, hands in the pockets of his jeans, the blue and white scarf knotted at his throat, an awkward smile on his face. He started to say, 'Hi, Mr Chapman . . .'

Dad cut him off. 'She's not coming out,' he said.

'Dad!'

He started to close the door. 'Get back upstairs, Angela.' He glanced up at me then did as double take. 'And take that muck off your face.'

Mark had put up a hand to stop the door shutting in his face. 'Please, Mr Chapman, it's not like we'll be out late.'

Dad was blunt. 'Look, son, get off home. She's not coming out and she's not seeing you any more. All right?'

Mark shot a desperate look at me. 'Please, Mr Chapman . . .'

I sat on the stairs crying, not caring if my mascara was running.

Mum came through from the kitchen. 'What's going on?'

'He won't let me go out!' My voice wobbled and more tears ran down my face. I must have looked a right state.

Dad gave Mum a warning look. 'I'm dealing with this.' He turned to face Mark again. 'Don't bother coming back. She's not seeing you.' He pushed the door shut.

I stared at Dad. 'It's not *fair*! Why *can't* I see him? I *love* him.' I was shouting.

Dad's lip curled. '*Love!* I've never heard anything so daft. Get upstairs – and *wash your face*.'

I flung myself on the bed and turned to face the wall. After a minute or two Mum came in and perched on the bottom of the bed. 'You know why you can't see him, Angela. You're far too young to be going about with a lad.' She sighed. 'You've been brought up a Witness. You know it's not what we believe.'

'Not what *you* believe, you mean.' I had stopped going to the meetings and I didn't want a boyfriend who was in the truth. That was just a way of keeping tabs on me.

'You shouldn't be going off on your own with a boy anyway, Angela,' Mum was saying. 'It's not right.'

'We're not *doing* anything.'

'You heard what your dad said.'

'I don't care. You can't stop me seeing him.'

Another sigh. 'Your dad's right, you know. In any case, you should be thinking about your school work, not mooning over some boy.'

16

Mark knew I'd been crying. My eyes were a mess, red and swollen, even though I'd dunked my face in cold water. We headed for the beach, arms wrapped round each other, and trudged along the promenade towards the pier. I needed a bit of time to calm down, otherwise as soon as I started talking I'd be in bits again and I didn't want that. I'd done enough crying already. I could feel the tears welling up and I dug my nails into the palms of my hand.

Mark kissed the top of my head. I shivered and did up the zip on my jacket. There were people on the beach, a couple with their coats on, huddling behind a striped windbreak while a skinny little boy in swimming trunks and an anorak with the hood up knelt on the sand and tapped the base of a bright blue bucket with a spade the same colour, turning out a row of sand pies. Something about the precise way he was lining them up made me think of Ian. When I was little we'd spend the whole day on the beach if the weather was nice. Mum would make a picnic of cheese sandwiches and hard-boiled eggs and she'd find a sheltered spot in the dunes with Becky, while me, David and Ian went off exploring rock pools, collecting shells we'd use to decorate enormous sandcastles.

The woman sat hunched up, a headscarf fastened under her chin, while the man leaned into the windbreak and cupped his hands round a lighter, trying to get a cigarette going. The tide was so far out you couldn't actually see the sea and the sky was grey, streaked with flashes of white, like the seagulls that were being blown about in the breeze.

We leaned on the railings and stared at the horizon.

Mark said, 'Did you know the tide here's really dangerous?' I slid my arms round his waist. 'Comes in so fast you can get swept away before you know it.'

I did. A few years before, wandering along the beach on a hot summer's afternoon with David, Ian and Rebecca, we'd almost got cut off. The tide had seemed a long way out as we trekked along the sand towards a bright yellow helicopter hovering on the edge of the shoreline. Before we got anywhere near a voice came through a loud hailer from the chopper telling us to go back and when I turned round the sea had sneaked in behind us, almost marooning us on a narrow spit of sand. I had picked Ian up and taken David's hand and we had waded back to safety. Two little boys who weren't so lucky were swept out to sea and drowned that day.

Mark gave me a gentle nudge. 'What's up, Ange? Has your dad had another go?'

I looked up and the wind whipped my hair into my face. Mark brushed it back and I tucked it into the collar of my jacket.

'Dad's been brilliant,' I said, and tears ran down my cheeks.

Mark was frowning. 'Why, what's happened?'

Snoopy, my guinea pig had died. She had seemed perfectly fine the day before when I'd fed her but when Mum went to give her fresh water in the morning she was dead.

'It's old age, Angela,' she had said, while I howled the place down. 'I mean, she must be getting on in guinea-pig years. She's what – six, seven? I don't think they live much more than that.'

Dad dug a grave in the back garden and put Snoopy in an old shoebox. He stood holding the makeshift coffin, me sobbing beside him. 'I know you feel bad,' he said, 'but we all have to go sometime and your mum's right – she's probably as old as guinea pigs can get.' He crouched down and put the box into the grave and gave me a smile. He had the kind of eyes that could change from violet to blue and sometimes grey. That day they were the colour of lavender. 'I bet she was at least a hundred on the guinea-pig scale of things. She should have a had a telegram from the queen.'

I managed a smile, glad he was trying to make me feel better. He shovelled earth onto the shoebox and patted the ground flat. 'Come on,' he said, putting an arm round my shoulders and squeezing. 'No sense standing out here feeling any worse than you already do. Just say your goodbyes.'

I pressed my fists into my eyes to stop the tears.

Mark listened as I told him about Snoopy, sobbing and hiccupping my way through the account of the burial. I dabbed a sodden paper hanky to my eyes. I couldn't stop crying. 'I feel so stupid getting this upset. I mean, she was only a guinea pig.'

'Yeah, but you'd had her years. No wonder it's got to you.'

'You must think I'm a right one.'

He held onto me. On the beach the man was rolling up

the windbreak and the woman was helping the little boy into a pair of shorts. The bucket and spade poked out of a wicker basket with a Thermos and what looked like screwed-up greaseproof paper and empty crisp packets – the remains of a picnic.

Mark nodded at the family. 'That'll be us one day.'

'Sitting in the cold on Cleethorpes beach!'

'We'll be making sandcastles, big ones with moats, burying the kids up to their necks in sand. Having tea out of a flask.'

'Heinz tomato soup.' I beamed up at him.

'See, you're feeling better already.'

17

I was desperate to start earning money and, through one of her Kingdom Hall friends, Mum helped me get a summer job in 1977 on the helter-skelter on the beach at Cleethorpes. Maybe she thought if I was working I'd be too busy to see Mark, not that it made the slightest bit of difference. We still spent every minute we could together. Mark would meet me after work and we'd sit on a bench on the promenade or hang about in the amusement arcade sharing a hot dog.

The helter-skelter was part of the tiny funfair that spilled onto the beach. There wasn't much to it, just a big wheel and a couple of rides with giant teacups and racing cars and whatnot for little ones, but I loved the atmosphere. There was always music blaring out – Donna Summer's 'I Feel Love' or Boney M's 'Ma Baker' segueing into blasts from the past like Mungo Jerry's 'In the Summertime' or 'Telstar'. The lads working on the big wheel, a long-haired laid-back pair in faded denims, seemed the height of cool to me. I would watch as they snapped the safety bars into place on the carriages, tipping up the ones that had girls in, making them scream, before they sent them soaring up into the air. It was a game. As the carriages spun round and the ride picked up speed and the screams got louder, they'd lounge against the rail next to the ticket booth taking not a bit of notice. One would almost always have a cigarette dangling from the corner of his mouth. They'd rouse themselves when the ride came to a halt and lend a hand to any pretty girl stumbling from a carriage looking a bit green. Compared to the big wheel my ride was tame, but we had plenty of takers, mainly kids, sometimes with their mums and dads, who loved climbing the narrow staircase and hurtling down the slide, tumbling onto the sand at the bottom. All I had to do was tear up tickets and hand out mats and I got £7 a week, which seemed like a fortune to me. At last I had a bit of spending money and started saving for the drainpipe trousers I'd wanted for ages.

It was 16 August 1977, a lovely warm day, and the beach was busy. The tide was about halfway in and there were people splashing about in the sea. Even though the sun was beating down I knew the water would be freezing. It always was. A young couple walked along the beach heading towards the amusements at the far end, leaving lines of footprints in the damp sand. An elderly man in a vest and trousers rolled up to the knees sat in a deckchair reading a paper. On a travel rug on the sand a couple of feet away, a younger woman played with a small, blonde-haired girl in a white cotton sunhat and pink swimsuit, making sandcastles that kept collapsing because the sand was too dry. They needed to get some from nearer the shore or fill a bucket with seawater and mix it to the right consistency. The little girl kept plucking shells from a pail and taking them to show the man, tapping on his paper to get his attention. In the end he gave up and put the paper away. On the promenade above me a couple leaned on the railings sharing a portion of fish and chips. Alvin Stardust was singing 'My Coo Ca Choo' and I was perched on a stack of mats at the side of the helter-skelter trying to get my face tanned. One of the lads from the big wheel ambled over and stood right in front of me, blocking out the sun. I blinked up at him.

'Heard the news?' Before I could say anything, he said, 'Elvis died.'

My jaw dropped.

His face gave nothing away. Being cool meant never showing whether you were bothered or not – even when it came to the death of a music legend. 'Overdose or something.' He kicked the mats with the toe of his biker boot. 'Shocker, isn't it?'

All I could think about was my dad. Elvis was his hero.

Mum was in the kitchen, bending over the sink, scrubbing at a stubborn mark on a baking tray. On the stove, a pan lid rattled and boiling water splashed onto the hob, almost putting the flame out. It flared yellow then turned a cool blue and Mum adjusted the heat, turning the gas right down. The lid stopped clattering. She shot me a warning look. 'Your dad's in the front room so don't go in.'

'Elvis died. One of the lads on the big wheel told me.'

She ran a damp cloth over the back of the cooker. 'Your dad's ever so upset, Angela.'

'Shall I say something?'

'Just leave him to it. He'll come round when he's ready.'

All afternoon I'd been thinking about those mad nights

when he'd come bounding in, full of it, and put one of his Elvis LPs on the radiogram, and get us all up dancing. Mum looked sad. I think we all felt Elvis going had taken a bit of something from us too.

18

Just over the road from where we lived in Cleethorpes was Sidney Park. I met Mark there and we sat on the swings, going back and forth, side by side, pulling them together so they twisted about as we tried to keep them moving. He got up and came to stand in front of me, put his arms around me, and held me tight. I slid my hands under his denim jacket and round his waist, and pressed my face into his body.

'I love you,' I said into his T-shirt.

'I love you too, Ange,' he said, giving me a squeeze. 'You look great.'

I was wearing my best dress, the first proper new one I'd ever had. It was red with blue and white polka dot sleeves and matching buttons running down the front. My friend Sandra, who lived round the corner from us, had the exact same dress. I'd nagged Mum for the money so I could get one too. In the end she'd given in and I'd gone with Sandra to Maddox Fashions in the precinct in Grimsby. I felt about ten feet tall walking round town swinging my Maddox Fashions carrier bag, letting everyone know I'd been shopping for clothes. Every time I put the dress on I felt different, grown up.

Mark said, 'I've got something for you.'

I looked up at him. He was giving me that smile, the one that turned my insides to mush. He fished something out of the pocket of his jacket and hid it behind his back. 'Close your eyes.'

I waited, eyes shut.

'You can open them now.'

He was holding a small padded box, the lid open to reveal a half eternity ring. I gazed at it. He took the ring from the box and slid it onto the third finger of my left hand. 'You know I want to be with you for ever,' he said, adjusting the ring so the row of white stones was dead centre. The gold band gleamed. 'I want to marry you. You're the only one, Ange.'

I stared at the ring. It was beautiful, the nicest thing I'd ever had. At home, there were never presents. Not on birthdays, not at Christmas. We'd have a bit of a knees-up for my mum and dad's wedding anniversary and that was it.

He said, 'Do you like it then?'

'I love it. It's perfect.' I knew we'd be together for ever and couldn't wait to get married, find a place of our own, and have kids. The fact I was fourteen made no difference. I was grown up enough to be working in the school holidays, earning money, buying clothes. I'd moved on from tearing tickets in half and handing out mats at the helter-skelter to a shop selling novelties further along the sea front, then a chip shop, serving at the takeaway bar to start with and then at tables for people wanting to eat in. I'd even served the singer Joe Brown before he did a gig at the Winter Gardens and got a massive tip. Things were looking up. I didn't mind working hard and I loved mixing with new people. I knew I wasn't going to be stuck at home for ever with my dad telling me what to do.

*

Mum was dishing out chops with boiled potatoes and green cabbage for tea. I slouched against the wall, waiting to give her a hand with the plates. 'Mind your dad, now,' she said, putting an extra chop on his plate. 'He's in one of his moods.'

Dad had come in from work, gone straight into the living room and shut the door. He could spend hours in there stretched out on the settee with the curtains drawn and the television on. We all knew better than to disturb him.

I put his tea in front of him.

'What's that on your finger?' Dad peered at the ring Mark had given me.

Mum sat down. David and Ian were already elbowing each other and messing about. She shot them a warning look as the table shook.

'It was a present.'

'You've got it on your wedding finger.'

I moved the ring a fraction, admiring the little stones. When the light hit them at a certain angle they sparkled like real diamonds. 'Mark gave it to me.'

Dad thumped the end of his knife on the table. 'That lad! What have I told you?'

I braced myself. 'I love him and he loves me—'

Mum cut me short. 'Angela, just eat your tea.'

I gave my dad a defiant look. 'I *love* him and I'm going to *marry* him.'

'Angela!'

Dad was on his feet. The salt cellar went over. He grabbed me by the arm and dragged me out of my seat. His face was a mask of fury. 'Have you heard yourself?

I've never heard the likes of it! *Marry* – you're fourteen years old. You're still a child. You think you know it all but you're just . . .' he searched for the words. 'You're still my *daughter*.'

'Get off – you're hurting me!'

'I'll do more than hurt you!'

He dragged me into the back garden, wrenched the ring off my finger and stomped off to the shed. When he came out he had a hammer in his hand.

'Dad . . .'

He dropped the ring on the path and brought the hammer down on it. 'Don't think you can come in here wearing rings on your wedding finger.' The hammer struck the ring again. I put a hand up to my mouth.

'Please, Dad, don't.'

He struck it another blow. The beautiful ring, my precious gift from Mark, lay on the path crumpled, bent out of shape. I started to cry. Dad brought the hammer down again and again. He was breathing hard with the effort of it. Finally, he straightened up and pointed the hammer at me. 'I'm not telling you again, Angela. STAY. AWAY. FROM. THAT. LAD.'

19

I set off for school, nipped into the park, put my make-up on, and headed in the opposite direction to Lindsey Road High to meet up with Mark at the cemetery in Beacon Avenue. I wasn't bothering with school much any more. Mark had already left and I hated it, thought the lessons were a waste of time. I'd had a fight as well with another girl and that was pretty much the last straw. I didn't even know who she was, just some girl in my year with spots and greasy blonde hair who came bowling up one lunch time and started mouthing off about my mum being in some kind of weirdo cult, saying it in a loud voice that made people turn round and look. It was no secret that I was a Jehovah's Witness. Every day, while everyone else filed into assembly me and the one Jewish girl in the school waited outside. While everybody else was doing RE, I had library study. Nobody even asked me why any more. They all knew about me not celebrating birthdays or joining in the Christmas stuff. What they didn't know was that I was falling out with Mum over the meetings and refusing to go any more. The whole religion thing seemed pretty pointless to me, all that singing and reading from the Bible for hours on end two or three times a week. I had better things to do. All the same, I wasn't going to stand around while someone else ripped my mum to pieces, no matter what I did or didn't think about being a Witness.

The girl had said, 'Your mum's one of those freaks who goes round trying to brainwash people on the doorstep.' She jabbed me in the chest. 'Weirdo.'

Without even thinking about it I lashed out and punched her. She staggered back and made a grab for my hair and pulled hard. I belted her in the stomach. The next thing I knew we were on the grass – the grass no one was allowed to set foot on – rolling about, kicking and punching. I heard something rip and then a man's voice bellowing. 'You girls! What do you think you're doing?' Someone got hold of me by the shoulder and yanked me onto my feet. It was the head of year, Mr Duffield, who patrolled the grounds during break and went berserk if anyone so much as trod on a blade of grass. When he lost his rag his face would go bright red and he'd manage to look mad and terrifying at the same time. He had one hand on me and the other on Spotty. Her face was red, there was a scratch down the side of her neck and her shirt was ripped. I must have done that. I dreaded to think what I looked like. I put a hand up to my head where she'd grabbed a handful of hair. As far as I could tell, it was all still there. Mr Duffield marched us through the crowd that had formed a circle round us and into his office. He was practically purple with rage. I was sure we were both in for a beating. Now it was over I could feel myself shaking. I had never been in a fight before, unlike my brothers who were constantly being picked on and beaten up at school. That usually stemmed from being Witnesses too. David and Ian weren't the types to hit back. There was nothing about them that made you think they could stick up for themselves. In fact, Becky, a couple of years younger than Ian, was better at giving the bullies what for than he was. It seemed horrible and unfair that kids could be picked on for their parents' beliefs.

'Two girls fighting on the school premises,' Mr Duffield said, eyes blazing, straightening the lapels of his brown tweed jacket. His tie, a woollen one, a couple of shades lighter than the jacket, was at an angle. 'Ye gods, it used to be the boys we had to watch out for.' He gave each of us a long look of disgust. 'Right – who started it?'

I could feel my lip throbbing as I told him what had happened, how I didn't even know the girl and she'd come over and starting saying all this nasty stuff about my mum. I admitted I'd lost it and struck the first blow. Spotty started to say something about how her mum reckoned the Witnesses were off their heads – a bunch of nutters that needed locking up.

Mr Duffield held up a hand to silence her. 'I am *not* interested in ignorant and bigoted views,' he said. 'You'll keep them to yourself from now on.' He jerked his head at the door. 'Go and get cleaned up, Angela, and in future remember what they say about sticks and stones.' I hesitated. Was that it? No cane? He turned his gaze on Spotty. 'We pride ourselves on being tolerant in this school. There is no room for bigots – and if you don't know what that means go and look it up. Now, clear off the pair of you.'

I was dreading telling Mum, but she was fine about it. All she said was that you had to feel sorry for girls like the one who'd picked on me. 'What a terrible mother she must have.' She had given me a weary look. 'I do wish you'd come back to the meetings, you know.'

*

I was desperate to leave school and start earning proper money. In the cemetery I held hands with Mark and rested my head on his shoulder.

He said, 'Have they said anything at school – about you not going in?'

I shrugged. 'Don't suppose they've noticed. Don't suppose they care.'

Mark rubbed my hand. 'I don't want you getting into trouble.'

'I'd never get to see you otherwise.'

My dad had banned Mark from coming to the house. I hated it, having to stay in my room, while he stood on the doorstep pleading with my dad to see me.

A couple of months earlier, in January 1978, after a night of gales and huge waves, Cleethorpes had flooded. The railway line was damaged and hundreds of people ended up in an emergency shelter. Our house in Brereton Avenue wasn't far from the sea wall and the street was under water. What saved us was that a few houses in the terrace, including ours, had been built on a higher level than the houses on either side. Steps led up to our front door and put us above the water level. Just a few doors down, water had poured into these houses, wrecking carpets and furniture. The morning after the storm, I woke up, looked out of the window, and there was a boat sailing down the road, which was under about three feet of water. It was utterly bizarre. The place was eerily quiet: no traffic, no one out and about, everyone trapped indoors. Later in the morning, a knock came at the door. Mark had waded through the waterlogged streets to make sure I was all right. It was like seeing a knight in armour galloping up to the door on a white charger. It was the most romantic thing that had ever happened to me.

Needless to say, my parents were less impressed.

I had started skipping school so Mark and I could hang about together during the day. We never had any money so it was either the park over the road – which meant there was a chance Mum might see us – or the beach, or, more often than not, the local cemetery.

'As soon as I can, I'll leave,' I said.

'What about your exams?'

'I'm not doing exams.'

I didn't see the point of a load of qualifications to find a job. I'd already worked in a shop, used a till, and done a bit of waitressing. I knew how to add up and work out change and I was good with people. I was confident I'd get a job.

When I got in, Mum was waiting for me. I took one look at her face and knew I was in big trouble.

'Where have you been, Angela? And no telling lies. I know you've not been going to school. Your teacher's been on.'

My mouth felt dry. I'd never even thought about the school picking up on all those crosses against my name in the attendance register and getting in touch with my parents.

'Just tell me,' Mum said. She looked thoroughly bewildered, as if she couldn't imagine how I could have been pretending to go to school, coming in, shrugging when she asked if I'd had a good day, and all the time skipping off somewhere else.

I guessed she had a pretty good idea I'd been meeting Mark. I might as well own up. 'I've been with Mark,' I said, twisting a hank of hair in my hand.

Mum jumped forward and slapped me hard on the face. My hand flew up to my cheek. 'What was that for?'

I was so shocked when she hit me in the face I stood up to her and tried to push her. She went mad and put her face right in front of mine. 'Where do I start? Telling lies ... Skiving off school ... Doing God-knows-what with that lad.'

Dad came in at that point, having heard the commotion. I backed away. 'We've not done anything.'

'Pull the other one, Angela, do you think we were born yesterday?'

Mum put a hand on Dad's sleeve. 'Let's hear what she's got to say, Ron.'

'And get another pack of lies? I've heard enough already.' He grabbed me by the hair. 'You're coming with me, young lady.'

'Ow, get off!'

He dragged me all the way to the police station, me crying, him muttering about how I'd really done it this time.

He shoved me towards the uniformed officer manning the counter and did his best not to shout. 'I want you to do something with my daughter. She won't go to school, playing truant the whole time, and she's running off to meet some lad. She's under age, by the way.'

The policeman, tall and bulky with short grey hair parted at the side, gave me a steely look. 'Is that right?' He leaned against the desk. On the wall behind him was a calendar and a clock with a plain round face and big, bold numbers. The second hand juddered as it moved across the face.

I smoothed my hair where my dad had just about yanked it out of my head. My scalp felt tender. I loved my hair, which was well past my shoulders, the longest it had ever been, and the kind of dark brown that sometimes looked black, depending on the light. I refused to look at the policeman while my dad ranted on about me being a handful, wild, driving my poor mum up the wall.

On a chair in the waiting room under a map of the British Isles and a poster telling motorists to clunk-click every trip a man in a smart navy suit watched the antics at the desk. When he caught me looking at him, he made a big show of checking his watch.

I wished Dad would stop going on.

'I can't control her,' he was saying. 'She'll have to go into care.'

I stared at him. He was bluffing, surely.

'I'm not having her carrying on when she's under age and that's an end to it.'

The policeman wrote something down and told us to take a seat. Dad wouldn't sit down, though, and paced up and down the scuffed tiled floor of the waiting area, furious. 'You've brought this on yourself, Angela,' he said, exasperated, while the man in the suit studied his shoes. 'You wouldn't listen. You will *not* do as you're told. Well, I give up, I do.'

Tears streamed down my face. I had nothing with me – no bag, no jacket. I wiped at my face with the back of my hand, making even more of a mess of my mascara. I wanted Mark, my knight in shining armour, to burst in and rescue me.

The policeman was saying something to Dad about getting me into a care home for the night and social services doing their best to place me, maybe in a foster home for the time being.

He doesn't mean it, I thought, the tears coming harder, as Dad nodded in agreement. He's trying to scare me.

Dad shook the policeman's hand and turned to me. 'You're a disappointment, Angela, you really are. Well, you're not my problem now.'

He nodded at the policeman and went.

That was the last I saw of him for six months.

20

The children's home was in a dilapidated old building in a part of Grimsby I'd always thought of as rough. I couldn't help thinking if I'd done as I was told I could have been at home in a nice part of Cleethorpes instead of moving into a dump with just the clothes I was standing up in. I hated my dad for treating me like some criminal. I hadn't done anything wrong. I didn't care what he'd told that police-man, I wasn't having sex with Mark. Tears sprang up and burned my eyes again. I blinked them away and gazed at the entrance with its worn carpet and off-white walls. The paintwork was chipped and marked and faded from being washed too many times. I felt totally miserable and more than a bit scared. A couple of lads a bit older than me came down the stairs and hung about in the hall staring and whispering to each other. They seemed to think some-thing was funny. Eventually, a woman in a sloppy navy jumper and pleated skirt, with mousy hair tied in a loose pony tail, showed me to my room. She said her name was Karen and she was on duty overnight if I needed anything.

The room had a high ceiling and a big sash window with a pair of limp brown curtains. There were two beds, both with pink candlewick bedspreads. One had a rum-pled look, as if it was already taken. Karen turned back the covers on the other bed to reveal salmon-coloured nylon sheets.

'This is yours,' she said. 'I'll get you something to sleep in, and a towel. The bathroom's down the corridor, third door on the left.'

She went away and came back with the kind of nightie my mum might wear – white, with mauve flowers, in some kind of furry brushed cotton. It smelled funny, like it had been at the back of a cupboard for years. I stood in the middle of the room arms folded, feeling sorry for myself, wondering how long I was going to be stuck there but not daring to ask in case this Karen person said the chances were I'd be there for ages.

Once she'd gone I checked my face in the mirror. No wonder those lads downstairs had been laughing. There were smudges of mascara under my eyes, eyeliner smeared across my cheeks. I looked a complete mess.

The bathroom was another high-ceilinged room, all white tiles, a rubbery grey floor, and too-bright strip lights suspended on chains. Along one wall was a row of white wash basins and, opposite, cubicles with toilets like the ones at school. The end cubicle had a bath, a big old-fashioned tub with stained enamel. On the floor was a tub of Ajax and a string cloth that had once been white.

I washed my face, using the only soap I could find, a big green bar that looked and smelled like it was meant for household use, and went back to my room. Still no sign of whoever was sharing with me. I whipped off my clothes, put the awful nightie on, and got into bed, pulling the covers over my head. The bed had the same slightly fusty smell as the nightie. Maybe it was the soap powder they used. I imagined living here and after a while everything getting that same odour so people knew you were from the children's home just by the way you smelled. I wanted to cry again.

The next morning I stayed in bed under the covers until I heard whoever had been sleeping in the other bed leave the room. Then I put on the clothes I'd been wearing the day before and went downstairs. There was no sign of Karen but a bloke in cords and a denim shirt said there was a social worker coming to pick me up. I found a chair where I could keep an eye on the front door and waited for the social worker.

Linda was nice, jolly with short, dark hair and the same kind of glasses that flicked up at the ends that my mum wore. She said she'd picked up my stuff and I was lucky because they'd found me a really nice foster family. She didn't say how long I'd be staying with them. I sat in the front of her Ford Escort staring at the dashboard, thinking about Mark, wondering when I'd see him again. *If.* I could run away. I might have to, depending what this foster family was like.

'It's not the end of the world,' Linda said. 'I know it might feel like it now, but you probably all just need a bit of breathing space.'

She turned into a private road with enormous houses. I peered out of the window.

'Told you – you've landed on your feet,' she said, slowing down and pulling up outside a sprawling detached property with a neat front garden and a drive with wrought-iron gates. It was seriously posh. I shrank in my seat.

'Come on, then, meet your new family.'

21

My foster parents were a schoolteacher and his wife, a serious and respectable-looking couple. Mr Pearson had neat grey hair, gold-rimmed glasses and a long, thin face. Mrs Pearson was short and plump with fair, collar-length hair worn curly. She had the same kind of gold-rimmed glasses as her husband. Their children, a boy, James, who was about a year older than me, and a girl, Julie, a year or so younger, were slim and pale-skinned with white-blond hair.

The house with its heavy furniture in dark wood, creaky stairs and floor-length curtains felt old and expensive. Even my room, which I had to myself, had a big ornate mahogany bed and the kind of towering chest of drawers I'd expect to see in an antique shop. It was all strange and not at all what I was used to, but I knew I had to at least try and fit in.

At home, there was always some kind of racket; the twin tub sounding like it was about to go into orbit, David and Ian fighting, Dad yelling or, on one of his good days, blasting out Elvis. Here, there was no shouting, no one tearing up and down the stairs. It was incredibly peaceful. James and Julie came in from school and got straight on with their homework in silence. I slunk off to my bedroom on the pretext of doing my homework too. Not that I ever did. I was still determined to leave without doing my exams.

Mr and Mrs Pearson agreed that Mark could visit but that we couldn't go off on our own. I didn't care, as long as I could spend time with him. My parents wanted to come and see me as well but I said no. I was still angry with my dad.

I didn't mind my foster home, apart from panicking when I was in the bathroom in case I'd forgotten to lock the door, but after six months I was ready to go home. I got my things together and Linda came to pick me up in her Ford Escort.

'Ready?' she said, before she started the engine.

I gave a shrug. Was I? As ready as I'd ever be. 'Suppose.'

If my dad thought putting me into care would make me and Mark break up, he was wrong. I was as mad about Mark as ever, and when I finally came home my parents, defeated, agreed to let me see him.

We were officially together. He called for me whenever he liked and no one told him to get lost. We could walk down the road with our arms round each other. It was still the innocent teenage love affair it always had been, just out in the open at last. We didn't have to hide away in the cemetery any more because it didn't matter who saw us. Mostly, we'd go to the park and sit on the swings, or take the dog for a walk.

Teddy was the latest addition to the Chapman household. He was like a doggy version of my guinea pig, Snoopy, with the same russet coat and an identical white stripe down the centre of his face. Teddy was a proper character, a loveable little rogue. He had a cute, quizzical face that gave no clue as to how naughty he really was.

Any chance he got he would run off. If someone came to the door, Teddy would make a dash for it and skedaddle. He had no road sense whatsoever and would shoot straight out in front of oncoming traffic. How he didn't cause a pile-up or get himself killed I'll never know. It didn't matter how hard we tried to keep him in, he'd find a way to get out, and he loved Sidney Park. Or at least he loved causing chaos, careering past mums and toddlers as they fed the ducks, sending the birds flapping onto the pond. Teddy would stand at the water's edge, tail wagging, barking happily while the ducks quacked in protest, and we – mortified – tried to catch him. Sometimes he'd hurtle out of the park and be off across the road on the other side, and an hour or two later one of the people from Queen Mary Avenue opposite would bring him home.

It was always stressful taking Teddy out because he saw walks as one more opportunity to misbehave. He didn't like being on the lead and had this way of stopping dead without warning, twisting his head, and slipping his collar. Before you knew it he was gone. He was so fast it was impossible to catch him. I'd stand, collar and lead dangling uselessly in my hand, while Mark sprinted across the park, Teddy dodging and weaving, tongue lolling, a big grin on his face. He could scent trouble at a hundred paces. On one of his madcap escape missions he was hit on the head by a cricket ball. Another time, a park worker had left the door of the aviary open while he worked inside. Teddy, seeing his chance, was in there like a flash, tearing round, barking, causing uproar. We always seemed to be apologizing for him. Even so, we loved him. Still, no one was surprised when one day he slipped through the open front door when Mum was paying the milkman and didn't come back.

'Go and look for him,' Mum said. 'He can't have got far.'

Me, David and Ian went out and scoured the park. A small child was throwing bread for the ducks. I watched warily, expecting Teddy to launch himself like a missile from the cover of a nearby bush but nothing happened. He definitely wasn't in the park. We trudged round the streets calling his name and asking people if they'd seen him. No one had.

The next day we went to school, heartbroken. Mum washed Teddy's bowls and put them away. She unhooked his lead from the back of the door and put it in a drawer.

Later, Mum was walking down Brereton Avenue and a red car coming the opposite way caught her eye. It was crawling along, as if the people weren't sure where they were going. As the car drew level, Mum looked up and, on the back seat, staring right back at her, was Teddy. Her mouth fell open in disbelief. She had to be seeing things. She turned and watched the car, the tips of Teddy's ears just visible through the back window. Too late, she started to wave but the car kept going and Teddy, standing up now, paws on the parcel shelf, watched her, mouth open, a big silly grin on his face. She was still in the same spot, trying to work out if she had dreamt she'd seen her missing dog sail past with a strange couple, when the car came back up the avenue a second time. She flagged it down and the woman in the passenger seat rolled down the window and said, 'We're looking for number 251. We've found this stray and that's the address on the collar.'

Teddy scrabbled about on the back seat trying to poke his nose through the open window. Mum had a sudden vision of him leaping into the front and out of the window and running off again.

'He's ours,' she said, trying to keep the panic out of her voice. 'That's our Teddy. Hang on, I'll get his lead – and you'd better wind that window up or he'll be off again.'

22

When I was in foster care Mr Pearson had sat me down and told me why it was important to stay on at school and do my exams. Mum and Dad did the same, but I took no notice. All I wanted to do was get a job and make some money so in 1978, when I was fifteen and without a single qualification to my name, I left school.

By the time I was sixteen I was working at Dot's Place, a greasy spoon in Riby Square in Grimsby, packed every day with dockers who came in for breakfast. Dot's was famous for its bacon and egg baps, and the blokes from the docks were generous tippers so I was making decent enough money. All the same, I knew I'd never get rich frying bacon.

An advert on television caught my eye. It said the search was on for Miss Yorkshire Television – the region's personality girl was how they put it – and that open auditions were being held at the Winter Gardens in Cleethorpes. It was the cash prize and the fact a car was up for grabs that caught my attention. All you had to do was turn up with a swimsuit.

For weeks, it seemed like every time I sat down in front of the TV the advert came on for the Miss Yorkshire Television heats. I couldn't stop thinking about the prizes. In my bedroom, I studied myself in the mirror. I didn't look anything like a beauty queen, nothing like the girls in the

Miss World contest anyway. They were all shiny and perfect and incredibly glamorous. I was nothing, not special compared with them. Plus, I'd never have the nerve to get up on a catwalk in my swimsuit and parade about in front of people. I couldn't think of anything more embarrassing. Then again, I wouldn't have to tell anyone what I was doing and at least if I gave it a go I might just win something.

I walked into the Winter Gardens with my swimming costume and a pair of high heels stuffed into my bag and almost turned round and ran back the way I'd come. The place was packed. There must have been hundreds of people there. The woman at the registration desk made a note of my name and said, 'Who's come with you then?'

I hadn't told a soul about Miss YTV. 'Nobody. I'm on my own.'

'Well, we've got a good turnout,' she said, handing me a numbered band to wear on my wrist. 'Must be at least eighty girls here.'

My mouth was dry. I had no chance.

In the changing area I sneaked a look at the other girls. They were all a lot more polished than I was, doing their make-up and styling their hair. The room smelled of scent and hairspray and something pungent that made me think of the chemicals you got in hair salons. For the second time in the space of less than half an hour I felt like doing a runner. I took a deep breath and a voice in my head said, 'Come on, Angie, you're here now, just give it a go.'

I glanced at the girl next to me. She was tanned, head to toe, with perfect nails, long blonde hair and full make-up. Her swimsuit was bronze and gold, beautifully cut to make the most of her long, slim legs, with a little gold belt that accentuated her waist. What on earth did I think I was doing? I'd never been confident, always been the quiet one, almost painfully shy until I met Mark. Mark – what would he have to say about all this? I felt my cheeks grow warm. I wouldn't tell him. I wouldn't tell anyone, ever. I rummaged in my bag for my swimsuit, a white halter-neck with a flower print, and my white stiletto shoes. Before I lost my nerve I got changed and had a quick look in the mirror. I looked nothing like the other girls. My body was whiter than white and the white swimsuit only served to make me feel even more anaemic-looking. I gathered up my hair and let it fall in waves on my shoulders. That would have to do. The other girls were touching up their make-up. I hadn't brought any with me. I slid on my wrist band. The state of my nails! Working behind the counter in a busy cafe meant I had no time, or money, for manicures. I sneaked another look at the girl in the gold swimsuit. Her nails were immaculate. The other contestants were starting to file through to the backstage area. I could just put my clothes back on and go, nobody would know. A head appeared round the door. It was the smiley woman from the registration desk. 'Come on,' she said. 'We're just about ready to get going.'

I had heard people talk about being so nervous their legs turned to jelly and I'd always thought it was just a saying, but as I waited for my turn to go on stage I could feel my limbs starting to dissolve. I watched the girl in gold. She could only have been a year or so older than me but she looked so poised and confident. As each girl went down the catwalk there was a roar of approval and

I realized that everyone else had brought along friends and family to cheer them on. All of a sudden I felt very alone. I heard my name being called and willed my legs to carry me. *Just once down the catwalk and back,* I pleaded with them. *Don't let me down, please.* My legs shook as I took my first few steps along a catwalk that seemed to have suddenly doubled in length. Just as well I didn't have to say anything. I'd never have got the words out.

I reminded myself why I was there. I wanted to make money, not have to scrimp like my mum had all her life. I wanted nice clothes, a car, holidays. My face ached with trying to smile. I dreaded to think what I must look like. I could feel my knees knocking as I turned and made my way back up, heart thumping, resisting the urge to run.

It was agony waiting for the results. All I wanted to do was slip away. Looking round at the competition, the dozens of glamorous girls bronzed and groomed to perfection, I wondered what on earth had made me think I could ever be a beauty queen.

The compere was saying, 'And the next of our ten finalists is . . . Angela Chapman.'

I was hearing things, surely. One of the other girls gave me a nudge. 'Go on, it's you!'

I went up on stage and joined the line-up of finalists. The judges had actually picked me – I couldn't believe it. The girl I'd been in the changing room with was there too, looking every inch a beauty queen in her shiny gold swimsuit. Her name was Della Dolan and her family had a business in Grimsby. She had a lot of support in the audience. I looked at Della and knew I had a lot of work to do before I did this again. Again! I was actually thinking about the next time. I'd need to put some fake tan on, learn how to do my make-up, get my nails done. The other nine girls in the line-up were toned and firm, no hint of flab anywhere. If I was serious, I'd have to make sure I stayed in shape since backless swimsuits with plunging necklines left little to the imagination.

In the hall as I was leaving, a woman came up and put a hand on my arm. 'Is this your first time?' she said.

It was that obvious. I nodded.

'You need more confidence, that's all. You're as good as any of the others. It's about how you present yourself. Shoulders back, chin up – you've got to sell yourself on that catwalk. Take a bit of time, pose for the judges.' I listened, amazed. 'Just have a bit of faith.' She looked me up and down. 'How tall are you?'

'Five seven.'

'It's a lot to do with grooming, looking the part. You'll get the hang of it.'

At home, I didn't tell anyone where I'd been. I knew I'd have to get to the *Grimsby Evening Telegraph* before my parents did, since a photographer had been at the Winter Gardens. For the next couple of days, I scanned the paper looking for the photo. When it appeared, it took up almost half a page, ten girls posing in their swimsuits, me right on the end. I hid the paper under my bed.

A few days later day Mum was in the back garden hanging out washing when the woman next door came out and said, 'Lovely picture of your Angela in the paper.'

Mum stopped what she was doing. 'Our Angela? In the paper?'

'Don't tell me you didn't you see it?'

'Well, I . . .'

'Not to worry, I kept it. I'll go and get it for you.'

Mum was shocked. Her faith meant she believed in modesty and thought parading about in a swimsuit was tantamount to shocking behaviour.

'What were you thinking?'

'I just wanted to have a go. You can win fantastic prizes.'

'A beauty pageant, Angela! I'd never have believed it.'

She had a point. I'd never thought of myself like that either. There'd been girls at school who were beautiful, the ones you could imagine being models. Everyone knew who they were and I certainly wasn't part of that crowd. I'd bumped into a girl from my old class on the bus the day after my picture was in the paper and the disbelief was written all over her face. I'd gone bright red when she'd blurted out, 'Was that really *you* in the paper?'

Mum said, 'I didn't think you were like that.'

I had surprised myself too. 'Mum, there were loads of girls and I got in the last ten. I've got a better idea what to do next time now.'

Mum looked utterly perplexed. 'Next time?'

Dad was thrilled his little girl had got her picture in the paper in a beauty contest line-up. 'I'll come and cheer you on next time,' he said, to Mum's dismay.

Mark grinned and put an arm round me. The *Grimsby Evening Telegraph* was open in front of us.

'You look great.'

'Not compared to the other girls.' I still wasn't sure what the judges had seen in me.

'You've every bit as good,' Mark said. 'I mean it, Ange.'

I felt a ripple of hope. If I worked at it maybe I could get on the beauty pageant circuit. There were loads of competitions; every seaside resort seemed to have one. That woman who'd come up to me at the Winter Gardens thought I had as good a chance as anyone. It had to be worth a go.

I didn't get any further with Miss Yorkshire Television but it had served its purpose. In 1980 I saw the girl in the gold swimsuit I'd shared a changing room with, Della Dolan, crowned Miss Yorkshire Television. The next time I saw her she was being crowned Miss England, then, in 1981, she became Miss United Kingdom. I watched in complete awe. She was a girl from Grimsby. Like me. She had started out in an open heat of the Miss Yorkshire Television competition. Just like I had. She was streets ahead of me now but her success made me think anything was possible. It was about having a dream and following it.

It didn't matter where I was from.

What mattered was where I was going.

23

It was 1981 before I entered my second beauty pageant and this time I had much more idea what I was doing. The pageant was in a marquee at the Lincoln Home and Leisure Show and the title up for grabs was Miss Lincolnshire. I had finally got the hang of applying fake tan after my first go with Sudden Tan left me the colour of a satsuma, streaky and stinking to high heaven. I'd worked out that the strange chemical pong backstage at the Winter Gardens when I entered Miss YTV came from all the girls being slathered in tanning products. I did my nails and put my hair in heated rollers to give it a big and bouncy Farrah Fawcett look. Already, I was about a hundred times more groomed than I had been at the Winter Gardens. I had a royal-blue halter-neck swimsuit with a belt and a shiny gold buckle at the waist. The show was set out like a garden fete with bunting and stands dotted around the edge of the marquee. Sit-on lawnmowers jostled for attention with camping gear, coloured flagstones and flowerpots, parasols and garden furniture that wouldn't have been out of place in a French bistro. It seemed to be a real family day out with plenty of children running about, playing in swish tents set up on fake lawns and queuing to clamber into the driver's seat of a silver Range Rover that had its tailgate and doors flung open. A hot-dog stall with a red and white canopy was doing brisk business and the whole place smelt of frying onions. I was wearing perfume, Tweed, which wasn't anywhere near strong enough to combat the scent of eau-de-onions. In the middle of all the hustle and bustle was the stage with its catwalk ready for the beauty pageant. By the time the competition started a good crowd had gathered.

On the catwalk I remembered what the woman who'd approached me at the Winter Gardens in Cleethorpes that day had said about making sure I kept my shoulders back and holding a pose. It still felt strange but at least my knees weren't knocking and I managed to keep my smile in place as I paraded up and down. This time I was much more aware of my surroundings and caught the eye of a woman wearing bright pink lipstick and an acid-yellow scoop-neck top with the kind of oversized shoulder pads favoured by Sue Ellen in the TV series *Dallas*. My smile widened. I loved shoulder pads too, the bigger the better. An image came to mind of how raw and unpolished I must have looked during the Miss Yorkshire Television heat and it made me smile even more. I'd worked out that success wasn't just about looking the part – it was about acting it too. The host was a local radio presenter called Phil Green, who had a look of the comedian Jasper Carrot about him. When he asked what my ambitions were I said I wanted to open a beauty salon. At the top of the catwalk, I posed one last time, back straight, chin up, aiming a bright smile at the judges. Next to Sue Ellen, a young lad in stonewashed jeans and a Fruit of the Loom T-shirt gave me a cheeky wink. I kept smiling. I knew I'd done my best.

Backstage, my stomach churned as the results were

announced and one of the runners-up was a girl who'd done a lot better than I had in the Miss Yorkshire Television competition. She had made it all the way to the final. It dawned on me I mustn't have been placed. 'And Miss Lincolnshire, 1981, is . . .' there was a buzz around the audience. I glanced at the other girls waiting with me. 'Angie Chapman.'

I laughed in amazement and went up on stage where the winner's sash was draped across my body and a tiara placed on my head. Holding the biggest bunch of flowers I'd ever been given, I floated on air along the catwalk, feeling a lump in my throat. I posed while photographers snapped away, waiting for it to sink in that I'd actually won a title. The prize money of £25 wasn't exactly going to change my life, but I didn't care. I was Miss Lincolnshire! I had well and truly caught the beauty pageant bug.

I started writing to tourist boards at seaside towns all over the north of England, asking for details of their beauty pageants. I'd get my stuff together and jump on a coach to places like Morecambe and Blackpool to take part. Mum still didn't approve, but she didn't try to stop me. With each pageant, I became more confident. I was doing okay, winning heats, picking up prizes here and there. If I heard about a pageant and it wasn't too far away I'd get the bus or hitch a lift from Mark on the back of his motorbike. We'd done a mad dash to Skegness one day for a competition at the lido. Somehow I'd managed to get my helmet on over my rollers and clung onto Mark's waist as we dashed the thirty miles or so south along the coast. I'd registered with seconds to spare and on the catwalk I told the compere about coming from Cleethorpes on the back of a bike and making it by the skin of my teeth. I think that helped me win the first prize of £100.

I loved the pageants. Often, on the judging panel there would be someone from a model agency, or a photographer, and I was starting to get offered some fashion work too. It wasn't enough to live on, though.

I had tried all kinds of jobs, even done a brief stint at the Findus factory. The work paid well and when I was offered a job doing quality control I took it. On my first day I was up at 4.30 a.m. to get to the factory in time for the early shift. I put on a white overall and hair net and took my place at the end of a conveyor belt. There were hundreds of women, all dressed in the same white overalls and hair nets, sitting in lines packing fish products into boxes. To me, the sound of the machinery whirring away was deafening. The factory was a vast, soulless place: no time for banter or a bit of fun, just endless boxes coming my way. It was my job to check each one and make sure it was properly sealed. After a day of doing that I was ready to climb the walls. The next day was a re-run of the first. And the day after. And the one after that. I sat at my station until the sight of packaged fish products sent me dizzy. My nana had worked on production lines in factories all her life. My mum had been a factory girl when I was little. I could not imagine how they'd stuck it. I thought about coming into work in the winter months when it was still dark outside, and leaving again in the dark, never seeing daylight. My nana was made of sterner stuff than me, no doubt about it. I lasted a week, collected my wage packet, and gave my notice.

Out of nowhere, when I was seventeen, my mum had announced she was pregnant. I could hardly take it in. It was the last thing I'd ever imagined, that Mum would have another baby. I couldn't get my head round it. All I could think of was her having sleepless nights and being up to her elbows in nappies again, just when the four children she already had were growing up and things had finally started to get that bit easier for her. She was always working, forever in the kitchen cooking and cleaning and doing the laundry, completely worn out as it was. Having another child had seemed mad to me, but she seemed perfectly happy about it. Now and then I wondered if I was set on the same course and that things would work out pretty much the same way for me as they had for her. The thought of it frightened the life out of me. I didn't think I was capable of doing what she had done.

I could tell Mum was worried about me doing the odd job here and there, never settling at anything. One day, she spotted a notice in the window of a stationery shop in Riby Square, just round the corner from where I used to work at Dot's Place. They were looking for an assistant. I applied and was called for interview. The shop was one of those old-fashioned posh places with gleaming glass cabinets filled with pricey fountain pens. Plenty of people were chasing the job. More than 180 had applied, it turned out. I thought the fact I'd left school without qualifications would count against me and at the interview they gave me a good grilling. Although I'd not done my exams all the other jobs I'd had meant I had plenty of experience when it came to dealing with customers. To my amazement, they offered me the job. Mum was overjoyed. I think she felt as if I was finally going to knuckle down and stop flitting from one thing to the next. It was a great opportunity, I knew that, but the more I thought about it the more I knew it wasn't for me. I didn't see my future working in a stationer's, never leaving Grimsby. When I turned the job down I don't think Mum could take it in. She probably thought I'd taken leave of my senses. I was adamant, though. I didn't want to stay in Grimsby for ever. It wasn't like I had a plan, a clear idea of where I was going and how I'd get there, but something told me to keep entering the beauty pageants and see where they took me.

24

I was working in a bar and doing a couple of nights a week waitressing in a restaurant and in between I'd see Mark. We'd been together since I was thirteen and now, more than five years on, I was starting to have doubts. I didn't get that rush of excitement at the thought of seeing him any more. My tummy didn't do strange little flips when he aimed that gorgeous smile of his at me. He was the only boyfriend I'd had and I was starting to wonder if I still loved him the way I had in the beginning. At the same time I thought that maybe what I was feeling was normal, just what happened to every couple. Years down the line, things were bound to feel more settled. I couldn't help worrying, though, that I wasn't even nineteen and already I was in a rut.

I sat with him in our local one night, lost in thought.

He squeezed my hand. 'What's wrong? You're miles away.'

'Just thinking.'

'Okay.' He shrugged and picked up his pint.

I looked at him. He hadn't changed much since I'd first met him: still the same long hair, the love of denim. His passions were Chelsea FC, heavy metal and me, not necessarily in that order. I knew he loved me. He told me constantly and I believed him. Years before, when we were still at school he had spray-painted our names and

4ever onto the side of a building. My poor mum had almost died with shame having to walk past it every day. For so long I had been head over heels in love with Mark, wanted to marry him, have his babies, live happily ever after. Ange and Mark *4ever*. Now I wasn't so sure. I was starting to wonder if this was how it would always be – the highlight of our week a trip to the pub for a couple of drinks. Chances were we wouldn't even be doing that once we started a family. I kept thinking about my mum working her fingers to the bone, always short of money, never having anything nice. Everything seemed a struggle, and it amazed me how she just got on with things and coped. I had no idea how she did it. For years the house had been in a state, open at the back while another bathroom was being put in. There wasn't the money to just get the job done and it had dragged on for an absolute age with Mum and Dad paying in stages and putting up with the mess in the meantime. Now there was another baby, my little sister, Anna. I wasn't at home much any more so I didn't see first-hand how things were. As usual, Mum managed somehow. I admired her so much and at the same time I knew the life she had wasn't for me.

I was ambitious, going out to work, earning money, trekking across the country to enter beauty pageants. I would tease Mark about dossing round at home while his mum ran after him. Increasingly, I felt as if the two of us were poles apart, although he didn't seem to see it.

He was fine with things the way they were, happy to stay in Grimsby for the rest of his life. The kind of domestic set-up my parents had, scraping along, would probably suit him down to the ground. The trouble was, it wasn't for me any more and the sooner I put him in the picture the better.

When I told him I wanted to break up he was shocked. 'I don't get it,' he said.

'There's things I want to do. I don't want to be stuck here.'

'So let's live somewhere else.'

'I think we should call it a day.'

'But Ange, I love you.'

'I know, and it's not you – it's me. I just want more.'

'What about getting married?'

'I can't spend the rest of my life here, I just can't. I don't want to. Mark, I'm really *really* sorry.'

We said more, lots more, and went round in circles for hours, but that's what it came down to. I wanted to end things and he didn't. I felt mean and rotten for breaking his heart and making him cry. I cried too, sobbed, because the dream we'd shared was over.

25

I met Melanie when the pair of us were waitressing in an Indian restaurant on Cleethorpes Road in Grimsby. She had arrived from Australia to see family and decided to stick around. Melanie had short dark hair and a lively, pretty face. She was funny and big-hearted and always up for having a good time. We clicked right away and it wasn't long before we decided to share a flat. For the first time in ages I started to enjoy myself and feel good about being single.

It was Melanie's idea to go on holiday to Spain. I had never been abroad but I loved the idea of going somewhere hot and sunny and coming back with a proper tan. I just didn't have the money. Typical of Melanie, she said she'd book us a package trip and I could pay her back later.

We flew from Manchester to Lloret de Mar on the Costa Brava. On our first day we went to sunbathe by the hotel pool. Melanie nudged me. 'This place is crawling with talent,' she said, her face lighting up. She was right. There were loads of good-looking guys and it wasn't long before Melanie got talking to a couple of them. Tony and Alan were from Manchester and it was their first time abroad too. It was obvious they were taken by Melanie's Aussie accent and the fact she had been halfway round the world on her own. Clearly, Melanie was the adventurous type, which might have been why they asked if we fancied going horse riding with them. I opened my mouth to say no but Melanie was already saying yes, we'd love to, that would be great. We arranged to meet them in reception that afternoon.

I was mortified. Horses scared me. 'What did you have to do that for?' I said, miffed. 'I don't want to go horse riding.'

'Oh come on, it'll be a laugh.'

'Really, I don't fancy it.'

'They're not going to put us on some crazy stallion or something,' she said. 'They'll just be nags for people who don't know what they're doing.'

'They can tell if you're scared, horses – they smell your fear or something.'

Melanie grinned. 'It's not a bucking bronco, Ange.'

At the riding centre the horses were huge. Mine towered over me, craning its neck to get a good look at the person daft enough to think she could ride it, showing the whites of its eyes, making me nervous. We were all in our holiday gear, me and Melanie in shorts and strappy little tops, the lads bare-chested. The sun beat down and we all wanted a tan. One of the Spanish grooms helped me into the saddle. Once I was up there I felt even worse. I was a long way off the ground. The horse tossed its head and shifted from foot to foot as I clung to the reins. I was so busy trying not to think what might happen if I fell off that I didn't see Tony trying to mount his horse. He had one foot in the stirrup and the other in the air when his horse took off, haring past me, dragging Tony along, shirtless, one foot still stuck in the stirrup, pursued by the stable lads yelling and grabbing at the reins. When I saw the state of Tony's back I nearly fainted. It was ripped to shreds, streaked with blood. Alan decided he wasn't going to get on his horse. I told the stable lad to let me down. Minutes earlier he'd been happily chatting in English. Now he pretended he couldn't understand. 'Get me down!' He gave my horse a slap on the rear and it set off at a lazy pace. I shot Melanie a look of panic but she was too busy hanging onto her mount to notice. Whether we liked it or not, we were going to have our ride.

'That's it, I want no more excitement,' I said when we were finally back at the hotel. 'From now on, I'm not moving off my sun lounger.'

A day or so later, I was minding my own business, slathered in sun cream and soaking up the sun at the side of the pool, when Hans loomed into view. Tall, blond, blue-eyed, with a handsome, chiselled face, he was my idea of a typical German. He put his towel on the lounger next to mine. Melanie sat up and started chatting. Hans spoke perfect English. You'd have thought Melanie had known him all her life. It was impressive how easy she found it to natter on with anyone who came into her orbit. I wouldn't have minded a dollop of her confidence.

Hans managed to keep his eyes on me as he kept up the chit-chat with Melanie. I gave him a smile. He brushed against my bare arm. 'So, how about we all go out later, have a few drinks?'

It was me he was talking to, I could tell.

Melanie said, sure, we'd love to, and Hans got up and swaggered off.

'He fancies you,' she said, watching him execute a perfect dive into the pool. He bobbed to the surface and gave us a wave. I waved back.

'He's all right, isn't he?'

'All right? He's gorgeous.'

I had only ever been out with Mark and it was strange being in a bar with someone else. Someone who obviously did fancy me. Hans bought me drinks, dragged me onto the dance floor, and put his arm round me as the night wore on. Melanie sipped her cocktail, something that seemed to have every white spirit going in it, and winked at me. At the end of the night it seemed the most natural thing in the world to go back to Hans's room. I didn't even disappear to the loos with Melanie first and ask her what she thought. I was feeling warm and fuzzy from all those lethal cocktails and, to be honest, it was nice getting all that attention from a drop-dead gorgeous guy.

Hans and I went back to the hotel, arms wrapped round each other.

The next morning, Melanie gave me a curious look. 'I don't see what the problem is.'

I dabbed at my eyes. 'I *slept* with him.'

She shrugged. 'Is that all?'

I couldn't stop crying. 'Some guy I don't even know . . .'

'You *do* know him. He's staying at the same hotel as us.'

I stared at her in horror. 'Oh God, I'm bound to bump into him.'

'Let's hope so, he's a bit of a looker, that one.'

I put my hands over my face. 'What was I thinking? I'd only just met him!'

'We're on holiday. Ange, we can do what we like.'

I had only ever been with Mark. I felt cheap, disgusted with myself. I didn't even know the guy's second name! 'I've only had one boyfriend,' I said, snivelling.

'Oh, is that it?' Melanie rolled her eyes. 'Listen to me. One boyfriend isn't nearly enough. It's about time you had some fun.' She looked thoughtful. 'I've had loads of blokes. Dozens.'

I gazed at her. 'Really?'

She started counting, using her fingers. After a few seconds, she grinned. 'I was going to add them up but I don't think I can remember them all.'

I started to laugh. 'You're kidding.'

'At a rough guess . . . probably fifty, give or take.'

My eyes widened. 'Fifty!'

She shrugged. 'No idea, but who cares? You're on holiday. You're supposed to be having a good time. So – *have a good time*!'

When she had finished I felt a lot better. I still couldn't face Hans, though. He kept hanging round, asking if I'd go out with him, saying maybe we could keep in touch after the holiday. He was a really nice guy but it was no good. In the end I had to tell him I didn't want to see him again – not because I didn't fancy him. It was just that I was so ashamed of falling into bed with him on the first night I couldn't look him in the eye.

Melanie thought I was mad.

26

I ran along the sea wall on the front at Cleethorpes, breathing hard, the theme from *Rocky* playing in my headphones. It was 1982 and I was determined to keep in shape. All the girls I'd seen taking part in beauty pageants had impressively firm bodies and no wobbly bits, which made me think they stuck to strict workout regimes. I couldn't afford to join a gym but pounding up and down the sea wall with 'Rocky' or 'Eye of the Tiger' blaring from the cassette in my Walkman, kept me pretty fit.

Melanie and I had moved into a little terraced house in Heneage Road and I'd got a job shampooing at a hairdressing salon not far from the old house in Buller Street. I was still entering beauty pageants, winning the Morecambe heat of Miss Great Britain and Southport's English Rose. I still kept tabs on Della Dolan, the Grimsby girl who'd started out at the same time as me and who, in 1982, had come third in the Miss World competition.

Everything was just about perfect until Melanie told me she was pregnant and wanted to have the baby back home. I couldn't imagine life in Grimsby without her. She was the one who'd made it such a laugh.

'What am I going to do without you?'

She gave me a hug. 'You'll be fine.' I wasn't sure about that. 'And you can always come and see me in Oz.'

'I will.'

I'd started seeing someone, a DJ called Derek from one of the clubs in Grimsby. With his flashy suits, pricey cologne, and never a hair out of place, he was about as different to Mark as it was possible to get.

I was coming home late one night with Derek, walking down Heneage Road hand in hand in the early hours, when someone shouted my name. I turned and saw Mark at the end of the road. I knew he must have been hanging about waiting for me. I just didn't know why.

Derek peered along the road. 'Who's that?'

'He's my ex.'

'Is there something wrong with him?'

Mark had come off his bike and was on crutches. He hobbled up the road towards us yelling abuse and threats. A light went on at an upstairs window. I cringed. 'Mark, stop it, will you?'

He shuffled towards us. 'Is that why you dumped me – for a suit?'

'Mark . . .'

Derek held up his hands as if Mark had a gun pointed at him. 'Look, mate, I don't want any trouble.' He took a couple of steps away from me.

I stared at him. Fat lot of use he was going to be. I ran off up the road, fumbled in my bag for my keys, fell into the hall and shut the door.

Outside, Mark shouted my name. He was getting closer.

I sat at the foot of the stairs waiting for him to give up, or for one of the neighbours to call the police. It struck me that if I stayed in Grimsby I'd never move on. There were too many memories, too much keeping me stuck in the past. I couldn't even walk past the wall Mark had defaced proclaiming our love all those years ago without feeling guilty for finishing with him.

Melanie was leaving, checking out as she put it. Maybe it was time for me to do the same.

One of Mark's mates had a van and I asked him to give me a lift to Leeds. At a beauty pageant I'd met a guy who ran a model agency in the city and he'd said he'd be able to get me some fashion and photographic work. I got my lift to drop me off on the edge of Hyde Park and I stood for a minute getting my bearings, the address of the agency scribbled on a scrap of paper, all my gear stuffed into two black bin liners. I stopped a woman and asked directions. She pointed at a row of imposing houses on the far side of the park and I set off, cutting across the grass, my heels sinking into the ground, lugging the bin bags, ignoring the curious looks of passers-by.

I didn't care what I looked like. I was in a new city, about to make a new start. I stopped for a moment and put the bags down. One was starting to rip. A stiletto heel poked through and I got a glimpse of my best red dress. My feet were starting to hurt.

I stood on the doorstep of the Leeds Model Agency, collar turned up, clutching my belongings. When the owner, Peter, came to the door, there was no mistaking the look of surprise on his face. His gaze dropped to the bin bags and he managed a baffled smile. 'Angie . . . what's brought you here?'

'I've moved to Leeds,' I said, keeping my voice bright. 'I've come to work. What have you got for me?'

His brow creased and he put a hand up to his chin. The look of surprise had become full-blown bewilderment. It hadn't occurred to me to call ahead and let him know I was coming. It was a second or two before he recovered his composure. 'Come in then,' he said, 'and let me take the . . . bags.'

I followed him into the reception feeling my confidence start to ebb away. Maybe it had been a bit rash chucking everything into bin bags and getting out of Grimsby as if the place was on fire. What harm would it have done to at least make a couple of phone calls first? What if I'd turned up and he had been out or the place had been all shut up? Peter disappeared along the hall that led to the back of the property. I sank onto the sofa. I hadn't exactly thought this through. Not so long ago it had seemed daring, jumping into a van and leaving my old life behind. Now, as Peter handed me a steaming mug of tea, I wasn't so sure.

'So, you've come to Leeds, permanent then,' he said. He paused for a couple of seconds. 'Have you got somewhere to stay?'

I opened my mouth to speak. I'd not thought that far ahead. I just expected to arrive at the agency and be put to work straight away. The rest, I supposed, would somehow fall into place.

'I take it that means no.' Peter crossed his arms. He was fifty-something with greying hair, his face etched with lines from years of experience. I wrapped my hands round the hot mug of tea and thought about how much money I had on me. How *little*. One night in a grotty B&B would probably be enough to clean me out. I realized I was pinning all my hopes on a model-agency boss I hardly knew. I took in his sensible jumper and slacks, relieved that he gave off none of the flashiness of some of the guys I'd met in the business.

He pulled at a bobble on his sleeve. 'You're one for surprises, Angie, I'll give you that,' he said, smiling and nodding at the bin liners. 'Is that all your stuff?'

'Yeah, I . . .' I shrugged.

I waited for him to suggest a cheap guest house and had visions of trudging back across the park with my belongings.

'Well, you can stay here until you get sorted – you'll have to sleep on the sofa, mind.'

He wasn't going to chuck me out then. 'Thanks, the sofa's great, and it won't be for long.'

'I can give you a bit of part-time work on reception until we start getting some jobs in for you.'

I had really fallen on my feet. I could have wept with gratitude. 'I'll start looking for a place soon, I will.'

27

I settled into a routine, doing a few shifts on reception at the agency, and got work serving part-time behind the bar at the Ritzy nightclub in town. Living at the agency meant I got to hear about jobs when they came in and, as promised, Peter put as much work as he could my way.

One day, out of the blue, he said, 'Can you dance, Angela?'

Before I'd left Grimsby I'd been in a dance group that met once a week at a church hall. There were only five of us, all inspired by the TV show *Fame*. Mostly, we did impersonations of pop stars. One of the lads, Steven, did a brilliant slightly off-the-wall version of 'Fade to Grey' by Steve Strange from Visage. He was a real star and we were all sure he'd be famous one day. There was a brother and sister in the group, Lorraine and another Steven, who performed as Dollar. I took off Kate Bush doing 'Wuthering Heights' and we had a routine we all did as a group to Imagination's 'Just an Illusion'. None of us had any formal training, we just loved getting together and rehearsing.

I told Peter I'd done a bit of dance, not admitting I'd never actually performed in front of an audience.

'There's a job in Hull,' he said, 'that needs a model who can dance. The money's good – £100 plus your travel expenses. What do you think?'

I thought I couldn't afford to turn it down even though

I wasn't sure I had the confidence to actually get up and perform on stage.

When I got to Hull the venue turned out to be a massive club packed to the hilt with a couple of thousand people. I could feel the nerves kick in when I saw the stage and the size of the audience. Heaven knows how I managed to get out there but somehow I did and my Kate Bush routine seemed to go down okay. The whole time I was dancing I concentrated hard on my moves and facial expressions and avoided making eye contact with anybody in the crowd. Afterwards, I was pleased with myself. I'd conquered a fear and been paid for it.

To start with in Leeds, I wasn't earning much, and when I looked for a place of my own all I could afford was a bedsit. After a few weeks dossing on Peter's sofa I moved into a place in Victoria Park Road, just a few minutes' walk from the agency. The house was awful, a filthy old Victorian place, divided into bedsits. The carpet in the entrance was clogged with years of dirt and in the hallway lining the walls were piles of newspapers stacked high. The landlord, a small, scrawny man in trousers that tripped him up and shirts frayed at the collar, had a habit of shuffling out from his ground-floor rooms whenever he heard a key turn in the front door. Every time I saw him I thought of the old man from the TV show *Steptoe and Son*. My room was up a few stairs at the end of a passageway. It was small and scruffy and had the same fusty smell as the lobby. I had a narrow single bed, a threadbare sofa, and a tiny little kitchen area with a sink and cooker. If I sat on the bed and stretched out my arms I could practically touch everything else in the room. I shared the bathroom, a couple of doors down. It was a squalid, depressing place but it was the best I could do. What really depressed me was that I'd had to ask the benefits office for help with my rent. I wasn't even earning enough to cover the cost of a poky little bedsit.

One day, I was letting myself in when the landlord popped up.

'There's been someone here looking for you,' he said, giving me a long hard stare. 'Some bloke with a briefcase.'

'For me? What did he want?'

He pulled a face. 'Wouldn't say. Said he'd be back, though.'

The next day I wasn't working so I stayed in just in case the man with the briefcase returned. Sure enough, about mid-morning there was a knock at my door. I opened up to find a tall man in a dark suit and overcoat in the hall and old man Steptoe hovering behind him. 'You've got a visitor,' he said.

The briefcase man was looking at me, huddled in layers of thick jumpers trying to stay warm, as if I wasn't quite what he expected. 'Miss Chapman?' he said.

I nodded.

'I'm from the Department of Health and Social Security. I just need a word about the rent you're claiming.'

I sat on the edge of the bed and he took the sofa, undoing the catches on his briefcase and pulling out a folder. He kept his coat on.

'What work do you do, Miss Chapman?'

I wondered what was going on. I'd never had to claim assistance before so I didn't really know what the procedure was. Perhaps house calls were normal. I told him about the part-time stints on reception at the agency, the bar job, how I was trying to build up the modelling side of things.

He frowned and leafed through his folder. 'I'm afraid we've had a tip-off that you're doing a lot better than that,' he said, handing me a sheaf of newspaper cuttings.

The top one was the front-page picture of me winning Miss Lincolnshire the year before. There were three or four others from seaside pageants where I'd taken second or third place, and a picture of me winning the Lincoln heat of Miss Cinderella Rockefella and going to the final in London. The girl who'd won that had gone on to be Miss England. I didn't understand. What did it have to do with anything?

'The press coverage seems to suggest you're doing quite well on the beauty-queen circuit.'

'I've done okay, nothing major.'

'According to these, you've won several cash prizes.'

I had. A few quid here and there. The most prestigious thing I'd won to date was the Miss Lincolnshire title in 1981. The picture of me beaming in my sash and tiara took up half the front page of the local paper. All I'd won, though, was £25 – hardly a fortune. Two years on and money was still tight.

'What, you think I'm rolling in it and still claiming for my rent?'

His face was grave. 'We have to investigate all allegations of fraud.'

My jaw dropped. Fraud! 'Do you know how much I got for winning this?' I held up the cutting from the Lincoln paper. 'Twenty-five quid! And that was ages ago. I've won the odd hundred quid, but I can promise you I've not got a fortune stashed away.'

'You do understand we—'

I cut in. 'Do I look like I'm making a packet?' I gestured at the tatty little bedsit with its shabby bits of furniture, wanting to cry.

'Well . . .' He glanced around the room, embarrassed. 'You certainly don't give the impression of living the high life.'

A couple of nights earlier I'd been woken by a mouse scuffling about. Whenever I put the light on it ran for cover and as soon as the light went off the scratching started up again. In the end I'd had to sit up waiting for it to show itself so I could trap it under an upturned waste basket and put it outside. I didn't imagine for one second that was the only mouse in the building. The place was probably infested. High life! I definitely wasn't living in squalor for the fun of it.

I bit my lip. 'Did someone send you that stuff and say I was fiddling the system – is that it?'

He looked uncomfortable. 'It does give the impression you're doing rather better than your circumstances suggest.' He held out a hand and I gave him back the cuttings. 'I don't think there's any need to take this further. I can see it's a misunderstanding.' He snapped the briefcase shut.

I saw him out and sat down on the bed again, tearful. Why would anyone want to report me when I was barely making ends meet?

Peter had got me a fashion show at one of the big night-clubs in Wakefield. It was modelling leather gear, really nice top of the range stuff – suits and trousers and funky little jackets. The place was packed and the show was a hit. Afterwards, I stayed on for a few drinks with a girl I'd met once or twice before on other jobs. At the end of the night she said her boyfriend would give me a lift home. I'd seen him around and knew him to say hello to but that was about it. He'd always struck me as pretty quiet. When we pulled up outside the flat he got out of the car and came to the door with me. 'How about inviting me in?'

'No. I mean, thanks for the lift but it's getting late.'

He gave me a funny look. 'Go on, the least you can do is make me a cup of tea for bringing you home.'

I leaned against the door. All of a sudden I felt woozy. I tried to keep my voice light. 'Not tonight, but thanks.'

He moved a step nearer. 'Come on, where's the harm?'

I didn't feel right. I fumbled around in my bag for my keys. I'd not had that much to drink, not enough to make me drunk, but the ground seemed to be shifting. I clutched my front-door key.

'Come on, Ange, a quick cuppa, that's all.' He was standing over me, too close for comfort. I took a deep breath. I knew I had to get inside. Alone. 'You'd better get home.'

'She won't mind.'

I shoved my key in the lock. No way was he coming in. 'Night then, and thanks again,' I said, raising my voice. I'd wake old man Steptoe if I had to.

'Suit yourself.'

I hurried in and shut the door.

I breezed into the agency the next morning for a stint on reception. Peter gave me a curious look as I slung my jacket over a hook on the back of the door. I sat down and flipped open the desk diary.

He came and stood in front of me. 'What happened to you yesterday?'

'What, last night you mean?'

'You were supposed to be here, doing a shift on the desk.'

I was baffled. 'I *was* here, then I did the show in Wakefield.'

Peter shook his head. 'Nope, don't think so. That was the day before.'

What was he talking about? 'I was in here yesterday,' I started to say.

'That would be Tuesday, then.'

'Yes.'

'So today's Wednesday?'

I frowned at him. I tapped the end of my pencil on the open diary. 'Yes, today is Wednesday.'

'I don't think so.' He picked up the folded copy of the *Yorkshire Post* that was on the corner of the desk and pointed at the date. 'It's Thursday today. You didn't show up on Wednesday.'

I grabbed the paper. If today was Thursday and I'd done the Wakefield show on Tuesday what had happened to Wednesday?

'Peter, I'm really sorry, I don't know what happened.'

He smiled. 'Good night, was it?'

I thought back to having a few drinks with my friend and her bloke and him bringing me home and how I'd suddenly felt drunk. I remembered him being pushy at the front door, wanting to come in, me saying no. I remembered letting myself into my bedsit and . . . I was a bit vague about how I took off my make-up and got into bed. I stared at the newspaper. I had gone to bed around 3 a.m. on Wednesday morning and had not woken up for more than twenty-four hours. I had passed out, slept right through the following day and night, and finally woke up a whole day later than I should have. My drink must have been spiked. No wonder that guy was so keen for me to let him in.

For the rest of the day all I could think about was what a narrow escape I'd had. The other thing bothering me was that I'd disappeared for a whole day and a night and nobody had come looking for me. I had no phone in the bedsit and the only person who'd ever called on me was the man from the DHSS. I felt horribly alone. The thought of going back to my depressing bedsit made me want to run home to Grimsby. I couldn't do that, though. Deep down, I was sure if I just hung on in there things would get better. What I wasn't so sure of was whether I could cope much longer on my own. It was one thing being strong and independent and another being lonely and miserable. It wasn't Grimsby I was missing, it was Mark. He had always stuck by me through thick and thin. Even my dad hadn't managed to scare him off. All of a sudden, he was the one person I wanted to see. I decided to get in touch.

28

Mark had stayed in touch after I'd left for Leeds, writing lovely letters. He was really pleased to hear from me and willing to up sticks and move to Leeds so we could be together. We found an airy first-floor flat on Headingley Lane in a rambling old house that was about a hundred times nicer than my bedsit. Mark got a job with a kitchen company and I was doing a fair bit of catwalk and photographic work and starting to build up a portfolio. It was 1983 and everyone wanted to get a foot on the property ladder. There was a lot of talk about renting being the equivalent of throwing money down the drain and we both thought it made sense to buy, even if it meant stretching ourselves, although much of Leeds was way out of our price range. On what we had coming in the most we could afford was a back-to-back house in Armley, not far from the notorious jail that dominated the area. The house and the neighbourhood reminded me of my parents' old house in Buller Street in Grimsby.

The house cost £11,000 and was like every other back to back. A front door opened into the main room with a partitioned area for the kitchen. At the back a narrow staircase led up to the bedrooms and bathroom. A second floor housed tiny attic rooms with sloping ceilings. Inside, the lack of light gave the place a dingy feel. It was a solid enough property, but I couldn't help thinking it was a bit of a dump. I tried to tell myself that owning a house – any house – was a good thing but every time I put my key in the front door my heart sank. The whole place with its dark, grubby-looking wallpaper and chipped paintwork needed redecorating. The carpets needed to be ripped out and replaced. The kitchen was antiquated. I pictured what it might look like renovated top to bottom but money was tight and we had to make do.

I had made it through to the final of the Miss Radio Aire contest at Casanova's nightclub in Wakefield and a friend had loaned me a blue strapless ball gown for the big night. There was a buzz around the contest. Radio Aire, a commercial station based in Leeds, was high profile and had put together one of the best prize packages I'd seen for a beauty pageant. There were clothes, jewellery, a year's hairdressing at a top salon, and, best of all, a car. All the girls had to go through an interview process and when my turn came I was ushered into a room to face the judges. It was quite a grilling with questions fired from all angles. I told them about wanting to visit Australia to see Melanie, how I was into fitness and weights, how much I loved being in Leeds. At one point a large woman with short dark hair asked me about the kind of work I was doing and I said something about promotions and building up a photographic portfolio. She said, 'How do you get to your assignments? Presumably you drive?'

I hesitated for a fraction of a second. 'Yes,' I said, 'I do.'

A couple of hours later I was on stage in the packed club adjusting the winner's sash, dizzy with excitement. I was Miss Radio Aire. I couldn't wait to tell Mark. The train back to Leeds seemed to take for ever and when I got home the house was in darkness. I let myself in, not caring how much noise I made. I was desperate to wake Mark up and tell him my news. I raced upstairs and burst into the bedroom.

'I've won Miss Radio Aire,' I blurted out, snapping on the light.

Mark covered his eyes and gave me a bleary-eyed smile. 'That's great, Ange.'

'I've won a car – a brand new Astra!'

He frowned and rubbed at his eyes. 'A car? That's fan— Hang on a minute, you can't drive.'

I gave him a manic smile. 'I know! What am I going to do?'

In fact, I could drive, it was just I hadn't passed my test. I'd had four attempts and every time I'd gone to pieces and messed up. I failed on something different every time. The examiner was spoilt for choice – poor clutch control, not using the mirrors, slipping back on the hill start, messing up the reverse parking . . . you name it. There was something about driving with an examiner, all stern-faced and not in the least bit friendly, in the passenger seat, that sent me into meltdown. Time after time, I was a complete bag of nerves, lurching and stalling my way through the whole miserable experience. Still, I refused to give up and a friend of mine, Elaine, who was also a model, would let me put L-plates on her car and drive the pair of us to jobs. Funnily enough, I was quite good behind the wheel as long as I wasn't taking my test.

Mark had sat up in bed. 'What are you going to do?'

I flopped down beside him. 'I don't know. I daren't tell them.'

I got on the phone to Elaine. It was gone two in the morning and she was half asleep. I said, 'I won Miss Radio Aire,' not managing to sound quite as excited as I'd been when I broke the news to Mark.

'What time is it?'

'Late. Sorry. Elaine – I've won a *car*!'

Silence, then, 'You can't drive!'

'I know. I'll have to tell them.'

'No!' She was suddenly wide awake. 'Don't tell them. Let's think . . .' I twisted the phone cord round my finger as dead air hung between us. 'I know, we'll get you to do your test again, see if they can give you a cancellation.'

'I'll have to tell Radio Aire.'

'No, do your test first.'

Elaine had a friend of a friend at the test centre on Harehills Lane and they managed to get me in at short notice. She took me out for practice sessions and made me do endless hill starts and three-point turns.

'See, you can do it,' she kept saying, as I manoeuvred with ease into a tight parking space.

'I don't drive like this when I do my test, that's the problem.'

'You just have to think positive. Think about what's at stake – that brand new Astra.'

On the day of the test I got into the car with an examiner with a face like granite. So much was riding on me passing that I was an absolute wreck. My body shook from head to toe. I seemed to have no control over my legs and I could see my arms juddering as I gripped the wheel. Sweat ran down the back of my neck. I was doomed, I knew it. I didn't need old granite face to tell me I'd failed. It was the worst feeling in the world. All I could think about was the shiny Vauxhall Astra with my name on it, still in the showroom waiting to be picked up. Well, with Miss Radio Aire plastered all over the sides anyway.

'Elaine, I've got to tell them.'

'No! We can . . .' she looked thoughtful. 'I know – we'll get a male model to pick the car up for you, make out like you've got a chauffeur, be a bit tongue in cheek. They'll like that. We can dress him up in a suit and one of those peaked hats and you can climb in the back. What do you think?'

I shook my head. 'I've got to tell them.'

It was the large woman with the dark hair who'd been on the judging panel I spoke to. She listened while I explained about having a provisional licence and not having passed my test yet.

'You're saying you can't drive?' she said.

'I can, it's just I've not got my test yet.'

'Angela, we need a Miss Radio Aire who can drive around in a car with our name on it promoting the radio station. You do understand?'

'Well, yes, I mean . . .'

'And you're obviously not in a position to do that, are you?'

'I do drive my friend's car. I put the L-plates on.'

'*L-plates?* I don't think that's quite the image we're looking for. I really don't see how this is going to work.'

I was crying. 'Can we not work something out?'

When they took the title off me and gave it to the runner-up I was devastated. In the space of a couple of weeks I'd managed to win a car and then lose it before I'd even got behind the wheel. It was too disappointing for words. It was a while before I finally passed my test – on the seventh attempt.

For weeks after the Miss Radio Aire contest I was in a slump, feeling awful, stuffing myself with food thinking that would cheer me up. I couldn't see the point of watching what I ate and trying to stay in shape any more. What for? I'd just seen the biggest prize I'd ever won snatched away. Chocolate became my best friend. I was putting on weight, but I didn't care and even managed to convince myself I had things under control. So I needed a few treats to get me through a bad time, so what? I was still in pretty good shape. That's what I told myself. I came to my senses one day when I was out shopping and took a dress into the changing room to try on. I knew my clothes were getting tight so I picked up a size 12 instead of my usual 10. I couldn't do the zip up. I tried on the size 14. The zip fastened but the dress was much too tight. I stared at my reflection in the harsh lighting of the cubicle, looking at myself properly for the first time in weeks, and I didn't like what I saw. I was practically bursting out of the dress. I turned and checked the view from behind. I had always liked having curves but now I looked positively plump. I felt like weeping. A few weeks, that's all it had taken to go up a couple of dress sizes. I had to get a grip or just give in and watch my weight balloon. I could see how easy it was for that to happen, how fast the pounds piled on, and how little effort it took. I straightened my shoulders and breathed in. I had heard about a diet where all you ate was brown rice. Some of the other girls said it was brilliant, that the weight just dropped off, and the guy who devised it claimed it was a fantastic way to detoxify the body.

For the next month all I ate was brown rice. That was my breakfast, lunch and dinner. The upside was that I could eat as much as I wanted so I never went hungry. The downside was that I was bored beyond belief. Still, the weight started to come off and I got back down to a size 10. The Miss Radio Aire fiasco had been a tough lesson, but there would be more competitions and gorging on chocolate was never going to improve my chances.

29

I had seen a competition in a magazine searching for a girl to be Miss Hawaiian Tropic. My eyes nearly fell out of my head when I saw that the first prize was a trip to Hawaii. I dug out a photograph of myself looking nice and brown in a white bikini and sent it off. A few weeks later I got a call to say I'd made it to the UK final at Studio Valbonne, a nightclub in London's West End. It meant a night in the capital at a plush hotel. Gabor, one of the photographers I knew through the model agency in Leeds, suggested I get an early train down so he could take me round some of the London agencies. 'You've got what it takes, Ange,' he said. 'We could hit the agencies before you do the competition – what do you think?'

The idea of modelling in London was both thrilling and terrifying. I'd only been down there a few times and it struck me as a scary place. All those people rushing about, bashing into you, giving you filthy looks if you didn't know where you were going. King's Cross station was like an obstacle course and the first time I was there I'd managed to step in front of a woman who was trying to bustle past. If looks could kill that would have been the end of me. Still, if I could get on the books of a London agency things could really take off for me, and maybe the capital was all right once you got used to it.

I had arranged to meet Gabor outside the station. As

soon as I stepped off the train I found myself carried along with the crowds. The place was heaving and I stopped next to the stairs leading down to the underground, trying to get my bearings. He had said to come out of the main entrance and wait just to the left of the main doors before the magazine kiosk. I picked up my case and headed outside where a mob was pushing its way onto a bus, everyone shoving. It made me shudder. I moved away from the door and put my case down. A voice said, 'Scuse me, can you just look after this for me?' I looked up at a guy with sunken eyes. He had a tatty denim jacket on and was already backing off, pointing at a big black ghetto blaster at my feet. 'Just keep an eye on it, won't be a minute.' I opened my mouth to object but he'd vanished into the crowd. I braced myself for a policeman to run up and tell me I was in possession of stolen goods. Oh, where was Gabor? Minutes ticked by. I checked my watch. I was early. Gabor would be another ten minutes yet. I thought about wandering off, finding a cafe, leaving the ghetto blaster on the pavement. Somehow, though, I didn't dare. The guy with the sunken eyes was back. He picked up his gear and gave me a grateful smile. His teeth were stained brown. 'Thanks for doing that, darling,' he said. 'Do you want to come for a drink?'

I stared at him. 'I'm m-meeting someone,' I said, stuttering.

'Well, I'm here and he's not.' He had the ghetto blaster across his front like a shield.

'No, no thanks, I'm . . .' I looked at my watch.

'I'm here if you change your mind, darling.' He gave me a cheeky grin. 'You know – if he stands you up.'

I watched him melt away again into the crowd, no doubt on the prowl for another green-looking girl he could dump his stereo on. Unusual chat up line, I'd give him that.

The first agency Gabor took me to was tucked away in the basement of a smart three-storey house with huge sash windows and cream-coloured wooden shutters. We had gone there on the tube, changing lines a couple of times, dragging my case up and down escalators. By the time we got to where we were going I was completely lost. 'Don't run off will you or I'll never find my way back.'

'Selfridges is that way,' he said jerking his head back the way we'd just come.

Knowing which way Selfridges was didn't help in the least. I still had no idea where I was.

We waited in reception. All over the walls were cover shots of some of the agency's girls on magazines like *Cosmo* and *Elle*. They looked extraordinary. A very skinny girl in a short denim skirt slouched in and took us into another room where a blonde woman was on the phone, scribbling something on a pad, then flicking through a diary and pushing her hair back off her brow. The girl who'd shown us in sat at a desk and started typing. Opposite her, another girl with a headset on was bashing away at a keyboard. On a leather armchair in front of the blonde woman's desk, a paunchy man sat with his legs crossed, his heel resting on the knee of his jeans. Gabor and I stood in the middle of the room, not sure what to do. I waited for the woman to come off the phone, tell us to take a seat, offer us a cup of tea. After what seemed a long time, she put the phone back in its cradle and looked up, frowning. She leaned on the desk and gave me a long, hard look. Then she got up and perched on the front of the desk next to the bloke in the leather chair. Her frown deepened.

'She's all wrong,' she said, eventually.

'Not tall enough,' the bloke in the chair said.

'Too fat,' the woman said. 'You won't get work with hips like that.'

I felt my smile slip.

'You could do with losing a couple of stone.'

'Her face isn't right,' the guy chipped in.

She peered at me. 'You've got too much make-up on.'

I stood there while they tore me apart. I had made a big effort getting ready that morning, doing my hair and make-up. I had on a little white fur jacket I'd got from a catalogue. In preparation for the Miss Hawaiian Tropic final I'd been on the latest faddy diet all the girls were talking about – Edam cheese and raisins. That was all I'd eaten for two days and I'd lost six pounds. My tummy felt flat. I thought I looked nice.

'Not for us,' the woman said, sitting down again at her desk, reaching for a pencil.

I had been in enough beauty pageants to be used to rejection. The difference was the judges at the pageants didn't sit there pulling you to pieces. No one had ever been so rude to my face. I struggled to keep my smile in place. There hadn't been so much as a hello, how are you, thanks for coming in.

I stumbled back up the stairs onto the street, not able to see where I was going because my eyes were filled with tears. Gabor put a hand on my arm. 'Ange, I'm so sorry,' he said. 'Don't take any notice.'

I blinked hard. I would not cry.

Gabor's face was etched with concern. 'If I'd known they were going to be like that . . . look, you're beautiful. Let's not give up. We can try somewhere else.'

'No, I don't think so.'

'Come on. Sod them. They're not the only agency in London.'

We got back on the tube.

At the next place the woman had cropped blonde hair and big glasses with thick black frames. She made me think of Brains from *Thunderbirds*. I stood there while she looked me up and down.

'Too curvy . . . too short . . . face all wrong.'

We trudged back to the street.

It was the same story at the next three agencies. I was not tall enough, thin enough, or beautiful enough. My look was all wrong. I would never succeed in London. I had brought a few fashion shots to show the bookers but I needn't have bothered because I never got the chance to take them out of my bag. No one was interested. Gabor kept telling me how sorry he was, how horrible they were, and that I mustn't take any of it to heart. He was right. My pride had taken a battering, but I could live with that. If that was the London modelling scene, they could keep it. Why would anyone want to work with people like that?

There was no time to wallow. In a few hours I had to be in the right frame of mind to stride down the catwalk in the final of the Miss Hawaiian Tropic contest.

Backstage at Studio Valbonne a team of make-up artists was getting us ready to go on. I was wearing my favourite frilly white bikini that looked great with a tan and I had a flower for my hair. Despite all the knocks from the agencies during the day I felt pleased when I checked my reflection in the full-length dressing room mirrors. If that was fat, it was okay by me. I didn't want to lose two stone and end up like that skinny girl at the first place we'd been to. She looked like she needed a decent meal, poor thing, but she could probably only get away with a bit of raw celery. I chuckled. I liked being in shape but for me that was a healthy size 10 with proper curves. Cutting down on what I ate for a couple of days before a competition was one thing but starving myself to get that emaciated look that seemed fashionable in London was quite another. I was glad Gabor had taken me round the agencies, because now I knew what it would take to succeed in London. Everywhere we'd been had seemed cold and unfriendly, run by the kind of people who appeared to have forgotten how to enjoy themselves. Lack of food, probably! In contrast, the beauty pageant world was fun. All the girls in the Hawaiian Tropic final were in high spirits, laughing and chit-chatting with the backstage team. There was a buzz about the place, a real sense of camaraderie. I ran a brush through my hair and swept it up on one side, holding it in place with the flower clip. One of the make-up guys came over. 'Let's just do a final check, darling, before you go out there and knock 'em dead.' He dipped a brush into a pot and dabbed peach gloss on my lips. 'You look great,' he said.

The club was packed, and walking down the catwalk that night with hundreds of people applauding was exactly what I needed to get over what had happened earlier in the day. I made it into the final group but it was an absolutely beautiful girl called Vivienne with long dark hair, piercing blue eyes and curves in all the right places that took the crown. I couldn't help wondering what that poker-faced lot in the agencies would have made of her!

30

It was only after moving into the Armley house that cracks started to appear in my relationship with Mark. He had always been easy-going, happy stretched out on the settee listening to Queen or one of his heavy-metal albums while stuff piled up around him, and now it was starting to grate on me. I would come home from work and find the place a tip, stuff everywhere. He'd leave dirty cups with the dregs of his tea on the floor and I'd come in and kick them over. I was turning into my mum, forever picking up and cleaning, trying to keep the place looking nice, but it was impossible to stay on top of things. I'd turn my back and there'd be another cup on the floor, the remnants of burnt toast all over the kitchen counter, tea bags on the drainer. I wanted to scream. I was having second thoughts about the wisdom of the two of us getting back together.

In the middle of all this I discovered I was pregnant.

My period was two weeks late and, fearing the worst, I had gone to a women's health advisory service in town for a pregnancy test. I sat on a hard-backed chair in the waiting room, flipping through an ancient copy of *Woman's Realm*, not managing to concentrate on any of the articles, praying I wasn't pregnant. There was a notice on the wall about contraception. It wasn't as if I'd not bothered. I'd been taking the Pill so surely I couldn't be pregnant.

'Angela Chapman?'

I went into a side room and sat at a desk facing a pale woman with blonde hair scraped into a severe ponytail. 'The result is positive,' she said. 'You're pregnant.'

I gripped the side of the chair and felt the colour drain from my face.

'I take it that's not what you wanted to hear?'

I shook my head. My mouth felt dry. I would probably never see this woman again but still I wanted her to know I hadn't been taking chances. 'I don't understand, I was on the Pill.'

'It's not a hundred per cent effective. Accidents still happen.' She searched around on the desk, gathering a sheaf of leaflets together.

'I'm not ready for a baby.'

'I can give you some information so you can think about your options,' she said, handing me the wad of papers.

It was October 1984 and I had just got back from working on the Rolls Royce stand at the Motor Show in Birmingham. For ten days I had been on my feet, smiling, posing for pictures next to the cars, and handing out brochures. Ours was definitely the swankiest stand at the NEC and it was a bit of a coup to be part of the Rolls Royce team. All the promotions girls had been auditioned in London and chauffeured in a fleet of Rollers to Harrods to be measured up for designer outfits. We all wore stylish navy suits and red blouses designed by the German fashion house Escada. The clothes were beautiful and had a price tag to match – hundreds of pounds for each outfit. There was a bit of a buzz around Rolls Royce and we all thought working for such a prestigious company would mean staying in the best hotel Birmingham had to offer. In fact, we were bused in and out each day from a modest little B&B about a forty minute drive away. Promotional work at the Motor Show meant long days on your feet in high heels, always smiling and looking your best. It was exhausting, but well paid. One morning, first thing, we'd been briefed that the Labour Leader Neil Kinnock would be visiting the stand. That same day, there was a bomb scare after someone left a briefcase in a car, and we were all ushered out while firemen and police officers streamed in. As the week wore on it was in the back of my mind that I should have had my period. I had never imagined I could be pregnant, though.

Mark was in no doubt he wanted the baby. I had already made up my mind that I couldn't have it. We had no money and were just about making ends meet as it was. How on earth were we going to manage with a baby and me not working? It made no sense.

I begged him to see things my way. 'How do you think we'll cope? It's hard enough as it is.'

'We'll be all right.'

I gazed around the poky living room, and had a vision of the future – forever scrimping, struggling, a house full of kids. It was the life my mum had. I shuddered. 'I can't do it. I can't have a baby. I'm not ready.'

'Ange, this is *our* baby we're talking about. We'll manage. People do.'

Not me. I had watched my mum go through so much hardship and heartache. All those rows in the kitchen with my dad about being hard up when they thought we couldn't hear. I wasn't about to do the same. I took a deep breath. 'I'm sorry, I can't do it. I'm getting rid of it.'

Mark stared at me. His face was white. 'Ange, you can't.'

'I'm really sorry.'

I ease back the covers and get out of bed, not wanting to wake Mark, who had nodded off almost as soon as he got his head down. His breathing is light, easy. I watch him for a minute, a shape in the darkness, completely still, no sign of the tossing, turning and throwing the blankets off I've been doing since we came to bed around midnight. It's gone four in the morning and I can't sleep. I won't, not now. For hours, I've lain awake, everything swirling round in my head, one thought crowding on top of another and then another, all jostling for space, until I feel as if there's no more room and I'm about to burst. I wish I could flick a switch and stop it. I get up and tiptoe across the room, pulling on my dressing gown, shutting the door behind me, taking care not to make a sound. My head pounds as I creep downstairs in the dark feeling sick, as if I'm coming down with something awful. I touch my forehead and feel it burning up even though the air inside the house is chilly.

In the kitchen I run the cold tap and wash down a couple of paracetamol with water, then lay a hand on my stomach. All I can think about is the baby and fighting with Mark and wishing I could tell my mum what's going on. I can't, though, because she doesn't agree with abortion and I know what she would say. What I really want is someone to tell me it's all okay, that there's nothing wrong with not wanting to have a baby when you're not ready.

My eyes swim with tears. In the days since doing the pregnancy test I have been absolutely petrified. The thought of bringing a child into the world when it's a struggle to look after ourselves is making me ill and nothing Mark says makes me feel better. He wants me to believe it will all be fine, that we'll cope. He's not scared, not like me. I lean against the sink, feeling my head spin. If the right thing to do was have this baby wouldn't I be feeling good about it, not filled with dread? Outside, the street is silent, everybody round about asleep. The rooftops opposite form a solid line against the blue-black sky. I shiver and pull my dressing gown up under my chin. You know something's right when it feels good and you know it's wrong when it feels bad – isn't that it? I feel terrible. I picture Mark sound asleep upstairs, as if there is nothing to worry about, and wish I could feel like that. I don't, though, I don't feel like that at all.

On the day I went to the clinic in Doncaster Mark came with me and all the way on the train begged me not to go through with the abortion. On the other side of the aisle a man in a grey suit, his coat folded on the seat beside him, made notes on typed sheets. I hoped he couldn't hear what we were saying. I felt dreadful. I could see how much Mark wanted the baby, but I had made up my mind. At the clinic I sat impassively as a woman talked me through the procedure. There was still time to change my mind. I couldn't, though. Wouldn't. Nothing anyone could say would have persuaded me to have the baby. The procedure was going to be done under general anaesthetic. I put on a gown and lay on the hard little bed waiting for them to come and put me under. Tears ran down the side of my head and into my ears. I wasn't just terminating the pregnancy; it was the end for me and Mark as well. There was no way back now. I knew he would never forgive me.

Back in Armley I got my things together and took a last look round the bedroom we'd shared. I was taking nothing with me apart from my clothes. Once I'd got myself sorted I'd sign over my share of the house to him. I was crying as I bumped my bags down the narrow stairs. None of this was his fault. He was still the same person I'd fallen for all those years ago. I was the one who had changed. There was nothing wrong with getting married, having babies, spending your life in a back-to-back house. Plenty of people did it and were happy enough. It just wasn't for me and, however much I hated hurting Mark, I knew I couldn't live a lie.

A couple of weeks after the abortion, in November 1984, I flew to Dubai for a series of fashion shows for Grattan's catalogue to celebrate British Week. I'd only told one person what had been going on at home with Mark and that was my friend Debbie, who was also on the Dubai trip. I was glad she was there because I needed someone to talk to and she let me pour my heart out.

'I feel terrible,' I told her.

'I know, but you have to do what's best for you,' she said.

'Mark only came to Leeds because of me . . .' my voice trailed off. I thought about him in the house in Armley and hoped he was managing okay. He had been in my life for so long and I'd loved him so much I couldn't just stop caring about him.

Debbie said, 'It didn't work, that's all. People break up all the time. If it's not right you can't stay with him, Ange. It's not fair.'

She was right about that. Sticking around when I knew it was over would have been wrong.

Debbie said, 'It's not the end of the world. I know it probably feels like it, but you just need to give yourself a bit of time.'

We spent ten days in Dubai and did a series of fashion shows. The audience consisted mostly of wealthy Arab men in traditional robes. After one of the shows the guy in charge of chaperoning us told me that a man in the audience had offered to swap a camel for one of the blonde models. I thought it had to be a wind-up, but he was deadly serious. We had been told that there would be royalty in the audience and it turned out to be Princess Anne and her then husband, Captain Mark Philips. After the show, in a corridor backstage, we got to shake hands with Her Royal Highness.

I wasn't sure what to make of Dubai. I had an idea in my head of somewhere exotic and far-flung with hot, dusty streets and bustling markets where nothing was sold without a huge amount of haggling. All I really knew was that it would take about seven hours on the plane to get there, which was the longest flight I'd ever been on. What struck me when we arrived was the heat – and the intense security. Everywhere we turned there were heavily armed security personnel. Our hotel was fenced off and ringed with gun-wielding guards, while outside our rooms there were men with guns round the clock. One day, sunbathing by the pool, I looked up and saw armed guards patrolling the roof above us. The security had probably been stepped up because of the presence of a member of the British Royal Family. I'd never seen anything like it and being surrounded by men with what looked like machine guns at every turn made me feel nervous and under siege. We spent most of our time inside the security cordon surrounding the hotel with the exception of one day when we went on a trip to the gold souk. We had all been told to cover up and everyone was modestly dressed in the searing heat, wandering around the market which had the biggest selection of jewellery I'd ever seen. As we browsed the shops, flanked by chaperones, I couldn't help noticing that we were the only women there. I had the feeling our little group must have seemed like aliens to the locals who gazed at us with what looked like utter fascination. None of it made for a relaxed shopping experience and I was glad to get back to the hotel and the grim-faced guard outside my room.

On 3 December we checked in at the airport for the flight home. Even in the departure terminal it struck me how much our group stood out. All around us were men in flowing robes. There didn't seem to be any women at all. For the whole ten days or so we'd been in Dubai the security and guns and chaperones had kept me on edge. Once in the air I reclined my seat and breathed a sigh of relief, glad to be heading home, unaware that behind us a drama was starting to unfold. The next flight out after ours was Kuwait Airways 221 bound for Karachi in Pakistan. As we cruised at 30,000 feet we had no idea it had been hijacked and was being diverted to Tehran in Iran. Needless to say, in Grimsby, my mum had caught something on the news about a plane being hi-jacked in Dubai and imagined the worst. She was just about frantic by the time I reached England.

'That could have been your plane,' she said, horrified, when things turned ugly and the bodies of hostages were dumped on the tarmac in Tehran.

The same thought had crossed my mind. 'I know but it wasn't, thank God.' I decided not to tell her about the rumours flying round that our plane, with royalty on board, was the one the hijackers' had really wanted. I didn't actually believe that but all the same it sent a shiver down my spine. 'The main thing is I'm home and I'm fine,' I said, 'so there's nothing to worry about.'

31

I met Sandra when we were both working as promotions girls at a motorcycle event organized by the National Coal Board. She was very pretty and bubbly with short dark hair. It was our job to present the winning riders with garlands and champagne. The two of us clicked right away.

'We'll have to have a night out,' she said.

'Yeah, we will.'

'Where do you live?'

I braced myself. 'I'm in Harehills.'

She gave me a look.

Harehills in the mid-eighties wasn't exactly the best area in Leeds. Not the bit I was living in anyway. After I'd split up with Mark I needed a place to stay and ended up in a tatty flat on a grim, rubbish-strewn street. When I went to look at it bad memories of my first shabby bedsit in Leeds on Victoria Park Road came flooding back but, having walked out of the house in Armley, I was in no position to be choosey. For a while I stayed with my friend Debbie and her family, but I needed to find somewhere long-term and it had to be cheap. That narrowed my options. The flat was on the first floor of a terraced house with blackened brickwork. Greying net curtains hung at the windows. There was a tiny bedroom with a single bed jammed up against a wall, a living room with a lumpy sofa, and a little galley kitchen with a gas cooker that looked like it needed a good clean. The bathroom had no window and a thin white shower curtain that was starting to go mouldy. The day I went to look at the place I wandered from room to room, pulling back the net curtain at the living-room window and sending a spider scuttling off up the side of the frame. On the other side of the road was a parade of shops with an off-licence, a bookie and a couple of take-aways. I fiddled with the fastening on the window and opened it wide. The remains of an old cobweb hung off the catch. The air in the street smelled of fast food. Behind me, in the doorway, the landlord, a bulky man in jeans and a checked shirt, hovered while I made up my mind. It was better than my old bedsit. Just. I let out a noisy breath, turned and nodded. 'I'll take it.'

I was getting used to people giving me odd looks when I told them where I lived. Increasingly, the crowd I was mixing with on the modelling circuit lived in what I considered to be the posh bits of Leeds: Alwoodley, Roundhay, Adel, Shadwell, Moortown. That's where all the parties were. Nobody seemed to live on my side of town. No wonder the flat had been cheap.

Sandra frowned. 'Do you like it where you are?'

I shrugged. No point in lying. 'It's a bit of a dump to be honest.'

She gave me a bright smile. 'Well, I've got a spare room,' she said. 'Why don't you move in with me?'

A couple of weeks later, I moved into an airy, modern flat in Moortown.

*

I was keen to keep adding to my portfolio of photographic work and Dollies Unlimited, an agency in Leeds, hooked me up with a photographer called Eric Cooper who needed a model for some fashion shots. Eric turned up at the agency with a few sample pictures to give me an idea of the kind of work he did. He spread his work out on a table, pushing a strand of curly brown hair off his face, as he outlined what he had in mind for the shoot we were going to do. I stared at the photos of a good-looking guy in a suit, tall and lean, with almost black hair. He reminded me of the Spandau Ballet singer, Tony Hadley, who I'd always had a bit of a crush on.

I tapped the corner of one of the pictures. 'Who's the model?'

Eric grinned. 'That's a mate of mine, Daniel, but he's not a model – he was just doing me a favour.'

My insides felt peculiar. Before I could stop myself, I said, 'I wouldn't mind meeting him.'

Eric laughed. 'Let's get this shoot out of the way first.'

Eric wanted to do the pictures somewhere quiet. We drove out of Leeds and he parked next to a dry-stone wall in the middle of nowhere. It was a lovely day, just a few straggly bits of cloud in a bright blue sky. The pair of us trudged across a field, me in high heels and a pair of leggings with stirrups and a gaudy pattern up the sides, Eric lugging his camera gear. He snapped away while I struck what I hoped were cool, moody poses. I was still learning when it came to the photographic side of things and I wanted to get as much experience as I could. I had no idea whether I was getting my facial expressions right, although Eric seemed happy enough.

I tilted my head on one side and gazed into the distance. 'Do you think I could meet your friend Daniel?'

Eric glanced up from the camera. 'Try turning your hip the other way. That's it.' The shutter clicked. 'You're bound to run into him,' he said. 'He's always around.'

'You could arrange it.'

Eric's hair flopped over his face. 'That's nice – hold it there.' The shutter went click click. He squinted up at the sky. 'Fancy coming to a party on Saturday? It'll be a laugh.'

I managed to stop myself from asking if Daniel would be there. 'Yeah, okay, that'd be great, thanks.'

32

I wore a white satin dress, fitted with shoestring straps, and a little kick pleat at the back for the party. My hair was down, falling in loose curls over my shoulders, and I had on a pair of silver platform heels with a peep toe. I'd done my nails bright tangerine. We drove up to a big house in Alwoodley and parked next to a red Golf GTI. Inside, the place was jammed with good-looking girls done up to the nines in skimpy dresses that showed off lots of bare, tanned skin, and guys in suits and open-neck shirts. Eric steered me to a corner and went to get drinks while I scanned the room for anyone I knew. There, in the opposite corner looking right at me was his friend from the photographs, Daniel. He must have seen us come in. My stomach went tight. He was even better-looking in the flesh. I couldn't just stand there staring so I weaved my way through the crowd and went up to him.

'You're Daniel,' I said, kicking myself, wishing I'd thought of something more original to say.

He smiled and I felt my insides start to dissolve. He gave me a long, amused look. 'Are you one of those psychics?'

We both laughed. 'I've been working with Eric, doing some fashion stuff. He showed me the pictures he did with you.'

'What – and you still let him do some of you?'

We laughed again. My stomach was in knots. Daniel started telling me he'd felt a proper Charlie posing. 'I blame him,' he said, nodding in the direction of Eric, who was on the other side of the room, a drink in each hand, talking to a short, balding guy. 'Eric twisted my arm, said he needed the practice.' He gave me another long look. 'I bet he had more fun working with you.'

'It was a right laugh,' I said. It had been too, although now I'd seen the pictures I wondered what on earth I was thinking wearing those awful leggings.

I just hoped Daniel wouldn't get to see those.

It didn't take me long to start falling for Daniel. He was my idea of the perfect boyfriend – really good fun to be with. We'd eat at nice restaurants and drink at the champagne bar at Mr Craig's nightclub. I felt as if I had stepped into a different world filled with ambitious high-achievers who knew how to have a good time. Sometimes I'd almost pinch myself thinking about growing up in Grimsby, wearing hand-me-downs, serving in a greasy spoon, doing a stint at a frozen-food factory – and wondering how, at twenty-two, I'd made the leap to what now seemed an incredibly glamorous and privileged life. Daniel moved with a smart and successful Jewish set that included a lot of the Leeds fashion crowd. The parties we went to were jammed with models and photographers and wealthy business people. At twenty-five, Daniel wasn't much older than me but he already owned some property that was doing well enough for him to have bought a big detached house in one of the best parts of town, Alwoodley. I was modelling, getting lots of photographic work – lingerie and sportswear and knitting patterns – in Leeds and Manchester, and still entering beauty pageants. I felt Daniel and I were made for each other, that the two of us were a perfect fit. Everything was working out at last and I couldn't have been happier.

In 1985 I decided to enter the Miss Cleethorpes pageant. I'd taken part three or four times before and always done all right in the heats but never come anywhere in the final. The title had never been won by a local girl so I wasn't holding out much hope. At the heats on the seafront I joined the line of girls parading up and down the pier. Holidaymakers clapped as dozens of girls clattered along in the sunshine in high-cut swimsuits and spiky heels, taking care not to lose a stiletto where the wooden floorboards didn't quite meet. Perfume and hairspray mixed with the smell of fish and chips and vinegar. The breeze was cool and as I headed along the makeshift catwalk a strand of hair blew across my face. I tucked it behind my ear, catching the eye of an elderly woman in a floral shift dress and quilted jacket, whose own grey curls were held in check by a see-through plastic rain hat. 'Poor lasses must be freezing to death,' she said, giving me a sympathetic look as I went past. I kept an eye out for the seagulls that hung in the air overhead, and dropped onto the roof of the pavilion, on the lookout for food. Below, the sea, grey and flat, slopped against the metal struts of the pier. I stood in the line-up, shoulders back, smiling, a hand on my hip, until the judges called my number. I was through to the final. Again.

I didn't bother telling anyone I'd got through the heats

to the final. There didn't seem much point since I didn't expect to win. The competition was indoors at the Winter Gardens on the sea front, scene of my first ever pageant almost six years before. A lot had happened since then. I knew how much difference a tan – fake or real – made. I'd learned to turn up to competitions with a vanity case bulging with make-up and hair stuff, just like all the other girls, and I no longer quaked with terror on the catwalk. In the run up to the final, I'd been on holiday to Ibiza and was nicely bronzed, and to set it off I wore a white halter-neck swimsuit with a little diamante clasp at the bust. I felt confident but, looking around, there were plenty of lovely girls there, any one of whom would make a worthy winner. Having been there several times before and come away empty handed I knew the score. No point in getting my hopes up. I took out my rollers and put a brush through my hair, arranging it in loose waves round my shoulders, and touched up my lipstick.

When my number was called I strode along the catwalk, posing for the judges, remembering how I'd scuttled off as fast as I could at the Miss Yorkshire TV auditions on that same stage a few years earlier. I had felt almost naked in my swimsuit then. Thinking about it made me want to laugh. When the host asked me what my ambitions were I said I wanted to go to Australia to visit my best friend, Melanie, in Queensland. I aimed a final smile in the direction of the judges, turned, and made my way back along the catwalk.

It seemed to take an age for them to announce the results. As the runners-up were called and I wasn't placed I was glad I'd not told anyone I was up for the title. I was just thinking about whether to go straight back to Leeds when they announced the winner and it was my name being called out. The other girls waiting backstage smothered me in hugs. I had actually won Miss Cleethorpes and no one was there to see it!

Afterwards, there was a party and I'd have loved Mum to come but I couldn't get hold of her. Dad, who was now driving vans for Mother's Pride, was at work but I left a message for him to come along later. Meanwhile, I managed to round up my Aunty Janet and Uncle Mick to help me celebrate. I'd won £450, which was a massive amount to me, the biggest cash prize I'd ever had, and I was the first local girl to win Miss Cleethorpes. When Dad turned up he was pleased as punch and the next day the two of us were on the front of the local paper, me with my tiara and sash, under the headline 'Father's Pride'.

The next day, I was back in my swimsuit on the beach posing for pictures for the *Grimsby Evening Telegraph*. The wind was bitterly cold and my smile was just about frozen in place. I could feel the cold seeping into my bones but the photographer kept going so I gritted my teeth. By the time he'd got all the pictures he wanted I was numb. The next day I came down with bronchitis and spent a week in bed, really poorly. Still, it was worth it because I'd finally won Miss Cleethorpes!

33

I was getting plenty of work, modelling swimwear for Arena, doing lingerie shoots for catalogues, and I'd landed a series of trade shows for a sportswear range made from Tactel, a new stretch fabric developed by ICI. I was thoroughly settled in Leeds, happy sharing the flat in Moortown with Sandra, and head over heels in love with Daniel.

Then things started going wrong.

I was waiting for him to pick me up one night to eat out at our favourite Chinese restaurant. I'd been away doing a fashion show in Gloucester, a corporate event for the ICI Chairman John Harvey-Jones and his wife, Betty, and hadn't seen Daniel for a few days, so I was really looking forward to catching up. I got ready, put on a short, strapless dress, made my hair really big, and dabbed Tramp behind my ears. I was expecting him at 8 o'clock and when it got to twenty past I started to worry. I tried calling him at home but there was no answer so I sat down to wait. He had probably been held up at work. It was no big deal. Then again, he could have called to say he'd be late. I stood up and smoothed my dress, which was starting to get creased at the back. I tugged at it and managed to snag my tights on my bracelet. Cursing, I rushed into the bedroom to change, certain the doorbell would go while I was still searching for another pair of tights. I got changed, checked my make-up, and went back into the living room. He was nearly an hour late. I dialled his home number again. No answer. I looked out of the window, hoping to see his car pulling into a parking space, but there was no sign of him. As the time wore on I started to imagine all sorts of things. I had visions of Daniel having a crash and being rushed to hospital. My mouth felt dry. It occurred to me that if anything did happen I'd be the last to know.

I had been seeing him for ages, nearly a year, but he had refused to take me home to meet his parents. According to his friends, they would never accept me because I wasn't Jewish. It didn't make sense to me and I really wanted to meet them, but Daniel wouldn't budge. Now, I sat with my stomach tying itself in knots, frantic with worry. By the time Sandra came in I was in tears.

Her face fell when she saw me. 'What on earth's the matter?'

I dabbed at my eyes. 'It's Daniel. He didn't turn up and I can't get hold of him.'

Sandra came and sat on the sofa beside me. 'What, he stood you up?'

I gave her a teary look. 'Something might have happened.'

'He might just have forgotten.'

'No, I mean, he wouldn't. We arranged it days ago. We were going out for dinner.' My brow creased. 'He said he'd book a table.'

Sandra frowned. 'Look, I wouldn't worry. Something probably just came up.'

'He'd have let me know, though.'

Neither of us spoke for a minute. Then Sandra said,

'It's probably nothing. Whatever it is, I'm sure he's got a good reason.'

It was days before I got hold of him. When I did he made light of standing me up. He said it was just one of those things and he'd gone out with his mates instead that night. He'd make it up to me.

'Don't mess me about,' I said.

'I'm not.'

'If you don't want to go out with me, just say so.'

'I do. Come on, Ange, don't make a big deal of it – it was just one night.'

It was a big deal to me, though, and I should have said so. Instead, I kept quiet.

He said, 'Am I forgiven?'

He was. I was mad about him and he knew it, which meant the chances of me putting my foot down were zero. From then on, the writing was on the wall.

34

In 1987, I went in for Miss Leeds Metro. It was a high-profile pageant run by the *Yorkshire Evening Post* and I really *really* wanted to win. I still felt I had something to prove after the Miss Radio Aire debacle. That whole experience had left such a bad taste and Miss Leeds Metro was a chance to put what had happened behind me for good.

The competition was held at one of the posh hotels in the city centre, the Dragonara, and among the dignitaries in the audience was the Lord Mayor of Leeds. The new Miss Leeds Metro would be joining him in an open-top limousine a few days later for the annual Lord Mayor's Parade. On the night, I went down the catwalk in a strapless floor-length gown covered in sequins with a big black fishtail that swished as I walked. When I made it to the final ten it sank in that I had a good chance of winning and I felt a little flutter of excitement. Even so, when my name was announced I was so thrown I didn't react and the other girls just about had to push me out on to the stage. Winning Miss Leeds Metro was such a big deal for me. I picked up a stack of prizes, including £100 in cash, a £500 holiday, clothes, a photographic session, and free hairdressing at a salon that was well and truly out of my price range. I also got to join the Lord Mayor on his parade, and went through to the final of Miss Yorkshire Television. Winning Miss YTV would have been the icing on the cake, since that was the competition that had got me started on the beauty-pageant trail, but when it came to it I wasn't on great form. Daniel had done one of his disappearing acts and I was all over the place. During filming, they asked about my boyfriend and I struggled to hide my feelings. That was it. I knew I'd blown my chances. I was twenty-four years old and decided I wasn't going to do any more beauty pageants. By then I'd won more than twenty titles ranging from Miss Bikini, Miss Lovely Legs, Miss West Yorkshire and Miss Cleethorpes, and felt like I'd achieved everything I wanted to. From arriving in Leeds with all my things in two black bin bags just four years before I had won the Miss Leeds Metro crown. I was ever so proud.

A few months later I was on one of the stands at the Harrogate Fashion Fair modelling samples from a collection all in leather and handing out brochures. The hall was stuffy and overheated and I felt warm in my tailored leather blazer. The annual fair was one of the biggest trade events in the fashion industry calendar. It was all about selling and filling order books and the stand had been busy all day. I must have had every garment on the sample rail on and off about a hundred times. One of my shoes, a sling-back with a towering heel, was starting to rub against the side of my foot. I just hoped my make up wasn't melting in the heat. A buyer stopped in front of the stand and gave me a long, curious look. I straightened my shoulders and held out a brochure, smiling as hard as I could at the tall, slightly tubby man facing me.

'I saw you in the paper,' he said. 'You're . . .' His brow

creased, as if he wasn't altogether sure. A hank of fair hair flopped over one eye. 'You're . . . Miss Leeds.' He sounded ever so posh. I gave him another smile.

His name was Ronald and he seemed more interested in me than the merchandise. He wanted to know where I lived, what kind of food I liked, if I'd ever been to the famous Box Tree restaurant in Ilkley and had I tried the Indian restaurant in Leeds where all the waiters dressed like Maharajahs. By the time he left he had talked me into going out with him.

The woman I was working for, a trim and glamorous forty-something in a black-leather pencil skirt and fitted jacket, could barely contain her excitement. 'You *do* know who that is?'

I didn't.

Her eyes sparkled. 'His family's got a chain of fashion shops.' She paused for effect. 'They own half of Yorkshire.' Another pause. 'He's *loaded*.'

I managed a smile. That explained the cut-glass accent. Still, loaded or not I was pretty sure he wasn't my type.

It was a couple of weeks since Daniel had stood me up yet again and I'd not heard a word from him since. We were supposed to have been going out for dinner in town when he had done one of his all too familiar disappearing acts. Not even a phone call. I had sat in the flat, all done up, trying not to crease my best silk dress, checking the time every few minutes, starting to feel my stomach churn, not wanting to believe he would make a date and then break it yet again without so much as a word. Half an hour after he should have been there I had called him and listened to the ringing tone drone on and on. I dialled the number again, carefully, in case I'd got it wrong the first time, and hung onto the receiver as it rang out. An hour and a half after he had been due to pick me up, I finally accepted he wasn't coming and went into the bedroom, took off the dress and put my dressing gown on. I was furious with him – furious and upset. Even so, a tiny nagging doubt ate away at me. I sat on the bed worrying, wondering if something awful had happened while I was thinking all these bad things about him. What if there'd been an accident or some kind of family crisis? What if he'd been on his way and got a flat tyre? That's what I wanted to believe: that there was a good reason for him not showing up, even though, deep down, I knew there was no point making excuses. The chances were he was out partying with his mates. There had been no accident, no crisis, no flat tyre. He was just behaving like a complete prat. I undid the straps on my gold shoes and put them away in the bottom of the wardrobe.

Ronald had invited me to a party at his parents' house, miles away on the other side of Bradford. He was dying to introduce me to his family. I decided to wear one of my beauty-pageant dresses, a pale pink taffeta off the shoulder ball gown with a frothy skirt and little puff sleeves. It was quite a job squeezing behind the wheel of my Mini Metro in that.

I had been in two minds whether to go. I'd only been out a couple of times with him and I knew there was no spark there, not for me anyway. It was hard telling him no, though, as he was a nice guy and obviously keen. A bit too keen. It had been my birthday a few days before, and first thing Ronald had called. 'Happy birthday, Ange! Go and look out of the window.' His voice practically crackled with excitement. I went and peered through the front curtains. My car was festooned in pink ribbon fastened in a giant bow across the bonnet. My jaw fell open. I watched as a van went past, a young lad hanging out of the passenger window, craning to get a better look. On the other end of the line Ronald was babbling. 'Go on, go and have a look, Ange. Your present's on the windscreen.'

There was a box, swathed in pink tissue paper, under one of the wipers. I picked it up. It felt heavy. I went back indoors and undid the wrapping. Inside, in a cream satin nest, was a Rolex, gold and shiny with a delicate, pearl face. I stared at it. I knew enough to know that Rolex watches didn't come cheap. I put the lid back on the box. I hardly knew Ronald. No way could I accept such an expensive gift. I got straight back on the phone.

'Do you like it?' He sounded out of breath and I had visions of him rushing about, setting up my birthday surprise, crawling about in the road in his suit, trying to pass the ribbon under the car.

I closed my eyes. 'Ronald, it's . . .'

'I wanted it to be perfect and when I saw it I just thought . . .'

'RONALD Ronald!'

There was a moment of silence.

'Look, it's lovely, really fantastic . . . but it's far too much. I can't keep it.'

'But I want you to have it.'

'I'm sorry, it's too generous.' I took a deep breath. 'We've only been out a couple of times.'

'It doesn't matter. I mean . . .' He sounded thoroughly perplexed.

'It does to me.' I was firm. 'You'll have to take it back.'

Neither of us said anything for a few seconds. Then Ronald, sounding resigned, said, 'You're still coming to the party, aren't you?'

I followed the directions to Ronald's family home, leaving Bradford behind, ending up on an unlit road, wondering if I'd taken a wrong turn somewhere. I was on the verge of doubling back when I spotted lights up ahead. I swung into a long, tree-lined drive that led to an enormous house and braked. Was this it? It looked like a stately home. I felt a shiver run down my spine. There were several smart cars parked at the end of the drive. I put the Metro into gear and crawled towards them, feeling a stab of anxiety, choosing a spot in the shadows, hiding my little car behind a gleaming Jaguar XJS. I knew Ronald's family was wealthy. The woman at the fashion fair reckoned they owned half of Yorkshire. I started to feel nervous, wondering just how formal and grand this party was going to be.

Inside, Ronald took my hand and led me through the vast entrance hall. There were paintings on the panelled walls, huge portraits of unsmiling people. I had a sudden memory of my dad and the landscapes he had found in the loft at Buller Street. Ronald steered me towards a woman with bobbed grey hair in a black evening dress. She was wearing lots of sparkly jewellery. I gazed at her necklace. The stones were probably real.

'Mother,' Ronald said, 'this is Angela.'

Ronald's mother smiled. 'Very nice to meet you, Angela,'

she said, taking my hand and giving it a squeeze that was barely there. She was even more clipped and well-to-do sounding than her son. 'Ronald has told us all about you.'

A young girl in a white blouse and black skirt sidled up with a tray of drinks. I took a glass of champagne and Ronald ushered me away. The place was filled with well-dressed, well-heeled people, huddled in groups, drinking and chatting and laughing. I had the feeling all the other guests were very much at home, that formal parties in the colossal piles of their friends was the norm. I drank some of my champagne and hoped I didn't look as out of place as I was starting to feel.

We ate in a cavernous dining room at a table covered in starched white linen, candelabra and elaborate flower arrangements.

'You look amazing,' Ronald said as waiters cleared away the prawn cocktail starters. He grabbed my hand under the table. 'Really beautiful.'

'Thanks,' I said, pulling my hand free.

'There's something I want to tell you,' he said.

He was giving me a big, soppy grin and there was a faint gleam of sweat on his brow. I was still on my first glass of champagne. I decided not to have any more to drink.

All through dinner, Ronald stroked my bare arm, leaned against me, draped an arm round my shoulder, said he needed to talk to me, to tell me something important. He was practically climbing onto my lap. I could hardly eat, he was making me feel so uncomfortable. I made up my mind to leave as soon as I could get away.

'Ronald,' I said, as we filed out of the dining room to

watch a firework display at the back of the house, 'I think I need to be going. It's a bit of a long drive back for me.'

There was a boom, and rockets shot into the sky, peeling off in different directions. 'I need to tell you something first,' he said, putting an arm round me. I shuffled sideways. Ronald held on tight.

A series of explosions sent streaks of green and white light into the night. 'Come on,' Ronald said. 'I need to talk to you.'

'It's time I was going home.'

He grinned. 'After we've had our chat.'

He was persistent, no doubt about it. I sighed and followed him back through the hall and up the stairs. 'Ronald, where are we going?'

'I just need a word in private,' he said, pushing open a door at the top of the stairs and stepping aside to let me go in first.

He snapped on the light. I looked around. We were in a bedroom. 'Ronald, look . . .'

He shut the door behind him. 'Angela,' he said, 'I've wanted to get you on your own all night.' He gave a helpless shrug. 'I just want to kiss you.'

I took a step backwards. 'I think I'd better go home.'

'But you can't, not yet.' He dropped to his knees. 'Just let me kiss you.'

I eyed the door behind him. 'I'm going now, Ronald – okay?'

He lunged at me and grabbed a handful of taffeta. 'No! I want you to stay.'

I pushed past him and rattled the doorknob. It wouldn't open. Ronald flung his arms round me legs. I pulled away.

My heart was thumping. 'Let me out, will you? I'm going home.'

'Please, Angela, just a kiss. Please.' Tears streamed down his face.

I felt a stab of panic. I was miles from home locked in a room with some guy I hardly knew bawling his eyes out. I banged on the door. 'Help!'

Ronald grabbed at my hand. I yanked it away. 'Get *off* me!' I hammered on the door again. 'Help! I'm locked in!' I could hear the muffled pops and whooshing of the fireworks still going off outside. No one was going to hear anything over that din. I wheeled round and glared at Ronald. 'Let me out – now!'

His face crumpled. 'I just want to *be* with you, Angela.'

I gave him a stern look. 'That's not going to happen. Now,' I put my hands on my hips, 'let me out before I scream the place down.'

Ronald clasped his hands. He was still slumped on the floor, shuffling about on his knees. 'Just a kiss, a little one, one kiss, Angela, please,' he burbled.

I took a deep breath and yelled at the top of my voice. 'Help! Help!' I thumped the door with both hands, making as much racket as I could.

There were voices outside and the doorknob began to turn. A woman said, 'Hello?' The door eased open. 'Tricky lock this one. What happened, lock yourself in?' Ronald's sister, who I'd met for the first time just a few hours earlier, stepped into the room. I clutched her hands, relieved. Her eyes went to her brother, weeping on the floor.

'Thanks ever so much,' I said, sweeping past her and down the stairs.

Outside, I started the car and sat for a moment waiting for my heart rate to steady. I was shaking. I backed out of my parking space and headed off down the drive, glancing in the mirror. There, running behind the car, dinner jacket flapping, stomach straining against his dress shirt, was Ronald. My heart rate shot up again. He lunged forward and yanked my door open. 'Angela, don't go! I need to talk to you.'

Not again!

I pulled at the door. Ronald pulled the other way. The car rolled forward. 'I'm going now,' I said, stating the obvious. 'Shut the door please.' He stuck his head into the car. 'Stop a second, will you?' His face was red.

I increased my speed as he jogged along beside me, hanging onto the door handle.

'Ronald, just let go.'

'I . . . just . . . want . . . to . . . say . . . something.' He was struggling to get his breath.

I braked hard and, shocked, he let go. I slammed the door shut and put my foot down, churning up gravel, catching the look of surprise on his face. At the end of the drive, I took a last look in the mirror to see him lumbering after me, too far away now to catch up as I accelerated off down the lane and out into the blackness. Behind me, rockets shot into the sky above the house.

35

Winning Miss Leeds Metro really raised my profile and I popped up a lot in the *Yorkshire Evening Post* attending different events. The coverage caught the eye of someone at Mecca Leisure and I was offered a job as promotions manager at one of their nightclubs. Confettis, with three bars, a staff of around fifty, and a capacity of 2,000, was one of the bigger clubs in Leeds. Being in charge of events there was an absolute dream job for me and for the first time in my life I was on a good salary. Much as I loved modelling the money was always patchy. Plus, with things between me and Daniel still up and down and all over the place, the idea of some stability in at least one area of my life was appealing. It was a good team at Confettis and I seemed to fit in right away. I was itching to get cracking and came up with an idea for a competition called Super Look to find the coolest and best-looking male and female clubbers in the house. I ran it along the lines of a beauty pageant, co-hosting it with one of the DJs, Terry George, whose monthly gay nights filled the place to capacity. Between us, Terry and I scouted the club for talent and ran a series of Super Look heats, him introducing the girls and me the boys, culminating in a grand final. It was the first pageant I'd run and I drew on all the experiences I'd had – good and bad – through my years of competing. I managed to get sponsors on board for Super Look and pull in a big crowd. By then, I had a pretty good idea what made the beauty-pageant world tick.

Not long after, a guy came to see me about running a Miss England heat at the club. Alex, short and tubby in a crumpled suit, was probably in his late forties and didn't immediately strike me as the kind of bloke who'd be running a beauty contest. I don't know what I expected – maybe someone in the mould of Eric Morley, in a dinner jacket and bow tie. I'd definitely been watching too many Miss World finals. Anyway, Alex was nothing like that. Between us, we staged the Miss England heat at Confettis and packed the place. It made me think I should run a Miss Confettis competition and that maybe one day running a Miss England heat on my own might not be beyond my reach.

I was fed up by then with Daniel standing me up so often. It had reached the point where I never knew whether he would actually show up when he was meant to and it was tearing me apart. More than once Sandra told me to dump him.

'He's not worth it,' she said whenever she found me all dressed up, mascara smudged from crying, after another one of Daniel's no-shows. Even though I knew she was right I just couldn't let go. For some reason I was totally hooked, convinced he was all I'd ever want. To me, Daniel was the be all and end all. Of course, he knew as much, and that's why he mucked me about, confident he could always win me round again when he was good and ready.

When Sandra moved out to live with her boyfriend, Holly, a girl I'd met at a fashion show, moved in. Holly was dark and pretty, level-headed and loyal. It didn't take long before she twigged what Daniel was doing – and what that was doing to me. Every time he left me in the lurch I'd be in bits for days.

'Just get shot of him,' Holly said. 'You can do a lot better than some bloke who doesn't even turn up when he says he's going to. You're wasting your time – he's never going to change.'

I was crazy about Daniel, though, that was the problem, and I believed him when he said he loved me. Then, just when I thought I couldn't take being let down any more, he asked me to move in with him. It was exactly what I wanted to hear and I jumped at the chance. But I was wary about having my heart broken, so when I moved my stuff into his house in Alwoodley I made sure I hung onto the flat with Holly.

Something told me I might end up back there.

Daniel's place was like a palace. It had three bedrooms, a state-of-the-art kitchen, and a lovely big sitting room that overlooked the back garden. He had done it out really well and bought some lovely furniture including an oversized settee in pale grey. It felt like a chance for us to make a home together, although I still hadn't met his parents and, deep down, I suspected I never would. Daniel's friends had made it all too plain that my not being Jewish would be a massive problem for his folks and whenever I brought up the subject with him he blanked me.

One Sunday morning, over a lazy breakfast of bagels and chopped liver, I had another go.

'I'd really like to meet your mum and dad.'

Daniel gave me an exasperated look. He finished chewing. 'Ange, I've told you, it's not a good idea.'

'We might get on.'

'Not if I tell them you're my girlfriend.'

I gazed at him. 'We're living together. I mean, it's not exactly a secret.'

He shrugged. 'They're really strict. '

I loved Daniel and I'd have married him like a shot if he asked me, but I wasn't so blind that I couldn't see there was little chance of us having a proper life together if I had to be kept hidden from his family. 'It's important,' I said. 'To me, anyway.'

'Can we just leave it?'

I decided I could just about live with not meeting his family, but what I couldn't put up with was his dog. Daniel wanted a guard dog to protect the place when we were out at work and that's where Tiger came in. He was a German shepherd, a big, slobbering brute that chewed everything in sight and shed hair all over the house. I watched in despair as he made himself at home, in no time at all behaving as if he ruled the roost. The lovely grey settee became a glorified dog basket. There were dog hairs everywhere and the place started to get that stale doggy smell. The stench of Tiger would hit me every time I came home. I'd get ready to go out and he would lollop over and jump up at me, leaving a trail of saliva on my dress or snagging my tights. I was always covered in dog hairs and I felt I couldn't escape the doggy pong. It got to the point where I didn't want to sit on the once-pristine settee, not after Tiger had been stretched out drooling on it all day. The house was going to wrack and ruin and

Daniel refused to do a thing about it. I put up with it for a few months, but it was never going to work now that Tiger had his paws well and truly under the table. He wasn't going anywhere so I had to.

I moved back in with Holly.

'Is that it, then, have you and Daniel finished?' she said, as she watched me unpack my stuff.

I gave her a sheepish look. 'It's the dog I can't stand, not him.'

Holly stood in the doorway, arms folded, as I moved around the bedroom putting stuff in drawers, hanging my dresses in the wardrobe. I held up my best red dress and showed Holly the stain on the front. She frowned. 'What happened there?'

'Tiger happened, slobbering all over me. I need to get it cleaned.'

'Send Daniel the bill.'

We both laughed.

'So it's still on with Mr Unreliable.'

'Suppose.' I'd had yet another go at Daniel about meeting his folks and as usual he'd blanked me. In my heart I knew things weren't leading anywhere, that we were going round in circles all the time, but I loved being with him. He made me laugh. He took me to nice places and made me feel special. Well, when he wasn't messing me about, anyway. I couldn't help how I felt about him. Holly wasn't the kind of friend to tell me I was wasting my time but from the look of concern on her face I had a pretty good idea that's what she was thinking. She wasn't the only one.

36

I kept seeing Daniel on and off, hoping that one day he would get his act together and show up when he said he would. It wasn't long, though, before things were back to how they'd been before and he was leaving me in the lurch again. Still we hung on. I don't think either of us was willing to end things once and for all. At least I had a job I loved and I'd made some good friends at Confettis. When Daniel did his disappearing act I could always offload to Tim, the manager, or Nick, one of the DJs, whose solution was nearly always to round up a crowd and go out on the town. Usually, I relied on work to take my mind off the hopeless state of affairs with Daniel. I was always up to my eyes in some show or competition. One night I was in the throes of a fashion show, checking through the running order, when I heard some of the girls backstage gossiping about a party they'd been to the weekend before in Alwoodley at some big house owned by a guy who was a dead ringer for Tony Hadley from Spandau Ballet. Straight away, my heart began beating a bit faster.

'Those Jewish boys are crazy,' a curvy girl with olive skin and dark hair said.

A tall willowy girl with a blonde urchin crop giggled. 'Wild,' she said.

I stared at my clipboard, the words and timings on the

page going blurry. I knew exactly who they were talking about. Daniel had stood me up at the weekend and when I'd finally tracked him down a couple of days later he'd shrugged it off, claiming he'd been out with a gang of mates.

The blonde girl said, 'At least I made it home. Unlike *someone* I could mention.'

My insides turned to ice.

The dark one said, 'I know, but he's gorgeous. Loaded, too. He's got his own business, you know.'

I kept my eyes on the clipboard where everything had turned into a jumbled mess that slid about on the page.

'Lucky cow. Seeing him again then?'

'Might do. He's got my number anyway.'

I forced a smile on my face. 'I couldn't help overhearing,' I said, doing my best to keep my voice light even though I felt sick. 'That guy you were talking about wasn't Daniel, was it?'

The dark one grinned. 'Yeah, Daniel. Do you know him, then?'

I managed to keep my smile in place. 'Sort of.'

'He's not got a girlfriend, has he?'

'Not as far as I know.'

Not any more anyway.

37

It wasn't long after I'd dumped Daniel – for good, finally – that the kind of opportunity that comes along once in a lifetime if you're lucky landed in Holly's lap. She was working part-time on reception at an old people's home and one of the residents had died, leaving a property. There was no family, no one to inherit, and eventually the only option was to sell. It was 1988, the asking price, at £12,500, was a bargain, and Holly got first refusal before it went on the market.

The house was a solid stone-built two-bedroom terrace in Chapel Allerton, not too far from the flat we were renting. It had been empty a long time and it looked like it. As far as we could tell, nothing had been done to it for years. The hallway was dark and grubby and at the foot of the stairs the wallpaper was starting to peel away, revealing what looked like brown watermarks underneath. I flattened a piece of swirly-patterned Anaglypta only for it to curl back on itself again. We wandered through the empty property, taking in the ancient sockets, the old-fashioned wire dangling from light fittings in the ceilings, the lack of central heating. The place was bone-numbingly cold. In the kitchen we weighed up the lopsided cupboards and the scratched sink and drainer under the window thick with dirt.

Holly peered into the sink and pulled a face. 'Oh God, is that a pair of teeth?'

I followed her gaze. 'Ugh.' The yellowing false teeth grinned up at us. We looked at each other. 'It needs everything doing,' I said.

Holly nodded. 'I know but it's such a bargain.' She linked her arm through mine. 'We could do it, Ange. It would be a laugh.'

'A laugh!' I opened a cupboard. A glass milk bottle with something green and veined growing inside made me take a step back. 'Oh my God, that's horrible!'

'Go on, Ange. We could do it all up and it would be *ours*. We'll make a bit when we come to sell it as well.'

I had got used to living in our nice, modern flat in Moortown with its piping-hot shower and heating that came on and off on a timer. Bad memories of the squalid bedsit I'd rented when I first came to Leeds flooded back.

'It wouldn't take that long to get it sorted,' Holly said, turning on one of the taps in the sink. There was a wheezing sound followed by a cough and then water spluttered out, drenching the false teeth.

'I'm not touching them,' I said, nodding at the teeth.

'We'll get a bloke in to do that.'

For five months we worked on the house, spending every weekend scraping away thick layers of wallpaper and cleaning up after the workmen who came in and replaced the wiring, fitted a new kitchen, ripped out the old stained bath tub ready for something new and shiny in its place, and took up sticky carpets. For weeks, the place was thick with dust and muck. We learned to make do, getting by on cups of tea and toast we'd eat standing up while the kitchen was out of action, relying on the showers at the gym when we had no bath. It was exhausting and every now and then we'd ask each other what on earth we were doing, but by the time we finished it was worth all the stress and strain because we ended up with a house that was perfect for us.

It was our dream to be pop stars so we decided one of the downstairs rooms would be a dance studio with a wooden floor and mirrored walls where we could practise routines. Things were starting to take off and we'd already done a recording session and laid down backing vocals for a band from Wakefield called Smokie, who'd had a hit a few years earlier with 'Living Next Door to Alice'. I'd sung lead vocals on the old Elvis Presley song that had been my favourite when I was growing up, 'Teddy Bear'. We were managing to get in the papers quite a bit. My being Miss Leeds Metro definitely helped. The *Leeds Weekly News* got behind us and ran a competition to find us a name, coming up with Incognito. Meanwhile, on the strength of the attention we were getting and the fact we were doing gigs in local nightclubs, Topshop agreed to sponsor us for clothes. We really thought we could go places.

At Confettis I was always on the lookout for ideas to bring in more business and a new TV show called *The Hit Man and Her* that was launched in September 1988 caught my eye. The show, hosted by Pete Waterman and Michaela Strachan, came from a different club every week. It was a slice of nightlife featuring DJs, dancers and clubbers. In the late eighties, Pete Waterman was just about the biggest name in pop with acts like Dead or Alive, Mel and Kim, and Rick Astley signed to the Stock Aitken Waterman label, but he was a real party animal too. He came to

Confettis a few times with the show and I always seemed to end up on the DJ podium dancing with him until the early hours. *The Hit Man and Her* was great exposure for the club. When word got out the show was coming to Confettis we had thousands of people queuing round the block. The place was crammed night after night. There wasn't always a featured band but we were lucky enough to get Sigue Sigue Sputnik, David Grant and Imagination, who'd had massive hits with songs like 'Body Talk' and 'Just an Illusion', and were as well known for their flamboyant front man, Leee John, as their music. He had the most fantastic clothes – glittering hooded jumpsuits, gold hot pants, glamorous one-shoulder tops. I seem to remember skin-tight sequined pants and some kind of jewelled collar that wasn't attached to anything and showed off lots of bare flesh. I made the front page of the local paper with Pete, and our resident dance group, Elite, became famous in their own right. I was blown away by the buzz of the music scene and determined that one day me and Holly would get our fledgling pop career off the ground.

In the meantime, I met Paul and everything changed.

Out of the blue, with things going really well at Confettis, I was offered a job with a London-based events company. I'd worked with them staging drinks and cigarette promotions at the club and knew they ran events at dozens of clubs all over the country. It seemed like a great opportunity. The guy who ran the company, Jeremy Taylor, was thoroughly professional and knew the business inside out. I was flattered he would want me to join his organization and arranged to meet him and his events team at a restaurant on Hanger Lane in London, to see if I would fit in.

One of the photographers, Paul, caught my attention right away. As soon as I walked into the restaurant he was on his feet, pulling out a chair.

'Come and sit next to me,' he said, fixing me with a broad, warm smile that went right through me.

I sat down and he eased my chair in for me, asked what I was having to drink and poured a large glass of chilled white wine. He kept his eyes on me. 'Well, Angela, you look absolutely amazing.' He shot a look at Jeremy sitting opposite, then back at me. 'So, when can you start?'

Everyone laughed.

Paul gave me a long, appreciative look. I picked up my drink. 'Give me a chance – I've only just got here.'

When I glanced back at him he was still gazing at me. 'I can't believe you've been hiding away in Leeds all this time.'

'Well, not exactly hiding.' I felt peculiar inside. For the first time since splitting up with Daniel I felt a flicker of attraction that took me completely by surprise. I took a hefty swig of wine.

As soon as I put the glass down he topped it up again. He couldn't take his eyes off me. 'I think you and me need to start making up for lost time,' he said. 'I mean, where have you been all my life?'

Jeremy caught my eye and grinned. 'Leave the poor girl alone. We don't want you scaring her off before she's even agreed to take the job.'

Paul, tall, with thick, dark hair and tanned skin, was nothing special to look at. He wasn't in any sense what you'd call classically good-looking, but it didn't matter because there was something about him that was completely charming. He was funny and charismatic and had everyone at the table in stitches all through dinner. I picked at my chicken madras, hardly able to eat a thing since my stomach felt so strange and knotted up. I knew what that feeling meant and I told myself to get a grip. I wasn't looking for anyone. All night, Paul let me know he only had eyes for me, leaning in close to ask if I was okay, making sure my glass was topped up. There were half a dozen of us round the table, but at times I felt as if it was just the two of us in our own fuzzy little bubble. He totally blew me away.

That night, I stayed at a Holiday Inn not far from the company's offices in west London. By morning, I was absolutely certain I wanted to be part of Jeremy Taylor's operation. The idea of running events on a much bigger scale than I ever could at Confettis and getting to travel up and down the country at the same time had me hooked. Although I loved the club and had some great friends there, it seemed the right time to move on. I had a new house I'd just done up with my best friend and now an exciting new job was in the offing. I couldn't help wondering if I had also found a new man. As I picked up my stuff from the hotel bathroom and packed things into my toilet bag I thought back to Paul the night before. He had managed to make me feel as if I was the only person in the room and it was a long time since anyone had done that. For more than a year Daniel had messed me about, not caring how hurt I was. I had cried so much over him, more than was good for anybody. Overhearing the girls in the club gossip about him still haunted me and made me wonder if all those times he'd claimed to have been with his mates he had really been with some other woman. *Women.* It made me feel sick to think of other girls staying at his place behind my back. He could have been lying to me and stringing me along for ages. I was never going to find out now. Meeting someone like Paul who was so obviously interested was exactly what I needed, or so I thought. I fished about in my make-up bag, found my lipstick, and slicked it on. In the bathroom mirror my reflection beamed back at me. For the first time in ages I looked happy, full of life.

Over dinner the night before, Paul had said he would drive me back to Leeds. It seemed crazy, completely over the top, and I tried to put him off.

'No, that's mad,' I said. It was hundreds of miles. I couldn't let him. 'You can't drive me all that way. Anyway, I've got a train ticket.'

'I'm going up north anyway,' he said. 'I've got an event not a million miles from you. You'll be doing me a favour, stop me getting bored on the motorway.'

'Are you sure?'

'Course – it'll be a laugh.' He gave me a look. 'I'd love to see where you live anyway.'

I had no idea how much my life was about to change.

38

The next day, cruising up the motorway, Paul got me talking about Leeds and doing up the house with Holly. I could tell he was impressed when I told him we'd renovated the place top to bottom in less than six months.

'You'll see it, anyway,' I said, as we sped up the M1 in his sports car. Cars like that certainly didn't come cheap.

He grinned at me. 'I can't wait.'

At home I started showing him round, telling him about the layers of dirt and the awful wallpaper and the teeth in the kitchen sink.

'How much did you pay for the place?'

'We got it for twelve and a half grand.'

He whistled. 'It must be worth a heck of a lot more now.'

I nodded, pleased with myself. 'One just like it went for forty grand not so long ago.'

Paul shook his head. 'Why don't you get someone round, tell you what you'd get for it? No point hanging on to it if you could make a killing just like that.' He rubbed his thumb and forefinger together. 'Got to strike while the iron's hot, Ange.'

'Well, yeah, I know . . . except it's our home. It's not like we did it up just to sell it. We want to enjoy it a bit first.'

He nodded. 'Course you do. Take no notice of me. Can't stop the old business brain ticking over.'

I opened the door into the room we'd made into a studio. Paul gazed at the mirrored walls. 'Well, you're full of surprises, Ange. I feel like I've just stepped into the Tardis or something.'

'It's where we rehearse, me and Holly – run through our dance routines.'

He gave me a curious look. I said, 'I told you we sing, didn't I?'

Paul frowned at me through the mirrored wall. 'Not everyone's cup of tea, though, is it, a rehearsal room? Might bring the price down when you sell, you know.'

I laughed. 'I told you, we're *not* selling. We've only just got it all straight so we're not going to want to move for ages.'

The next day a huge bouquet from Paul arrived at the house with a little note to say it had been great meeting me. I was still putting the flowers in water when he called to ask if I fancied going to Leicester at the weekend.

'What – this weekend? You mean, the day after tomorrow?'

'What's wrong – can't you wait that long?'

I laughed. 'You're full of yourself!'

'I don't know if *I* can wait. I might have to jump in the motor and shoot back up to Leeds.'

'Don't you have any work to do?'

'I can always tell them I'm sick.' He laughed. 'I am – I've got this pain, right in my heart. It's your fault.'

I couldn't help laughing at his cheek. 'Not sure you'll get away with that one.'

'Come on – you can see where I live, meet my folks if you like.'

I pressed the phone to my ear. All the time I'd been with Daniel I'd wanted him to take me home, show a bit of commitment, and instead he'd mucked about and gone off with some other girl – more than one, for all I knew – behind my back. Paul's enthusiasm was blowing me away. It was an amazing feeling to have met someone who fancied me and didn't mind saying so. We'd clicked, so what was the point in playing things cool? A tiny voice in my head told me to slow down and take my time. It was only a few months since Daniel had broken my heart and it might be an idea to keep this new guy at arm's length. I didn't really know him, after all. Then again, he was part of Jeremy Taylor's team and it was obvious how much they thought of him. His colleagues had practically been queuing up to tell me what a great guy he was. I took a deep breath. 'Okay,' I said, 'I'll come.'

From the word go, Paul let me know he was completely mad about me and in no time at all I was falling for him. I had never really understood before what it meant to be swept off your feet. It was like one of those tides at Cleethorpes that come in so fast they catch you off guard before you can do a thing about it. If I had stopped to think I would have known it was all happening much too fast but I was so carried away by Paul showering me with gifts and flowers and telling me how much he loved me that I hardly had time to catch my breath.

I phoned Mum to say Holly and I were selling the house in Leeds and that I was buying somewhere in Leicester with Paul.

He had found a newish three-bedroom semi-detached place that was immaculate. 'It's really lovely, like a show home,' I said.

Mum hesitated. 'It's all very fast, this, Angela – you've only known him five minutes.'

'I know but this place we've seen – we don't want to lose it, and it makes sense to be in Leicester. We need to be central for all the travelling we've got to do.' I was echoing what Paul had said about the merits of moving away from Leeds.

'You're sure about him, are you?'

When Mum had met Paul she had been bowled over by him too, just like everybody else. She had teased me, saying he was almost too good to be true. 'What's the catch then? He must have some faults.'

I had said, no, he was pretty much perfect.

Now I was beginning to have my doubts. A few weeks earlier, he had come to stay for the weekend and had picked a fight over Holly and me wanting to be pop stars. As he lay sprawled on the bed watching me do my make-up, he said, 'Aren't you a bit old for all that pop stuff?'

I bristled. I was only twenty-six and didn't feel in the least bit old. I said, 'We're getting offered gigs so obviously other people don't think we're past it.'

He pulled a face. 'Yeah – gigs in crappy clubs. Big deal.'

I coated my lashes in mascara. 'I'd have thought you'd be pleased.'

He shook his head. 'What makes you think anyone's interested in a beauty queen who's past her sell-by date?'

I turned and stared at him. 'Thanks very much.'

He stretched and put his hands behind his head. 'I'm

just saying, Ange, why would you want to get on stage at some dive full of drunks, all those blokes leering at you? I mean, it's not like you're ever going to make it.'

I rummaged in my make-up bag for blusher. 'We've recorded some stuff so we know we can sing.'

'The bloke at the studio probably fancied you.'

I checked my eyebrows. 'Stop being horrible.'

He gazed at me through the mirror. 'And I don't know why you wear all that rubbish on your face.'

I stopped what I was doing and looked at him. 'I want to look nice, that's why.'

'It makes you look cheap. You don't need all that slap on for me. We're going for something to eat, not to one of your *beauty contests*.'

The way he said beauty contests felt like a punch in the face. I snapped shut my compact and turned to face him. 'You know what – I'm not hungry any more. I'll see if Holly fancies doing something instead. You do what you like.' I hadn't even got as far as the door when he leapt off the bed, grabbed my wrist and yanked me round to face him. I nearly lost my balance.

His face was tight and furious. 'Don't walk away when I'm talking to you.'

'Let go, you're hurting.'

He dropped my wrist. I stood rubbing it. 'What are you playing at, Paul?'

He wiped a hand across his face. 'Sorry, Ange, sorry – I'm just wound up about the house and moving and all that and . . .' He gave me a helpless look. 'I hate it, not being with you.' He took hold of my hand. 'I've got a ton of stuff on my mind and I'm on the motorway all the time.

I'm bloody knackered, not that I'm making excuses. I shouldn't take it out on you. I don't mean to. I love you.'

'No, you bloody shouldn't.' It wasn't the first time Paul had lost his temper over something trivial. He wanted my undivided attention and if he didn't get it he flipped. Any hint that I might have plans to see friends when he wasn't around sparked an outburst. I didn't like the way he got rough, pushing me out of the way or giving me a shove when he lost his rag. My wrist where he'd grabbed it was sore.

When I had told Mum what was going on she wanted to know if he was hitting me.

'No, I mean, it's not like that. He'll just get hold of me a bit too hard, that kind of thing.'

She was in no doubt. 'If he's doing stuff like that now, Angela, it's only going to get worse. I'd get rid of him if I were you.'

Now, on the other end of the line in Grimsby, she sounded anxious. 'I hope you know what you're doing. All this rough business, pushing you around – I don't care what he says, it's wrong.'

I didn't want to worry her so I said, 'Mum, everything's fine, really,' even though I knew she was probably right. Paul had never actually hit me but I hated the way he shoved me out of the way when he was in a mood or pinched my arm so hard it left a mark. And I hated his little digs too, poking fun at me for being a beauty queen, saying I was past it, an old has-been. Although I'd called it a day with the pageants after winning Miss Leeds Metro I was proud of my past. I'd won a stack of titles in the eight years or so I'd been competing and I knew I owed my job at Confettis to the Miss Leeds Metro crown. It was the only reason they had heard of me and head-hunted me for the job of promotions manager. In a way, if it hadn't been for winning that final contest I'd probably never have met Paul. You'd think he'd have been happy about that, not constantly having a go, telling me I was over the hill. Holly had caught him at it one day and I saw the look on her face. Although she wasn't the type to say anything, I had a good idea what she was thinking. Of course, Paul went out of his way to make light of things, saying he'd only been pulling my leg and didn't mean anything by it. Later, when it was just the two of us, he had said he was sorry and what he meant to say sometimes came out all wrong.

'I'd never hurt you, Ange,' he had said, stroking my hair. 'I love you, you're beautiful. I'm just rubbish sometimes. I don't know what I'd do without you. We'll be okay once we get moved into our own place.'

The way he looked at me I knew he loved me and I felt bad because I also knew he was feeling pressurized and was lashing out at me because I was the person closest to him.

It would be fine once we were in the new house.

The house in Leeds wasn't on the market long before it was snapped up. My share of the proceeds – more than £10,000 – was going straight into the Leicester house. It was all happening so fast there was no time to stop, reflect and wonder if I was actually doing the right thing. Thinking about it, that was probably exactly what Paul wanted.

Terry George, the DJ from Confettis who'd run the

Super Look competition with me when I first started there, organized my leaving do. He had formal invitations printed and told everyone it was a black and blue ball and to come dressed only in those colours. I wore a blue pencil skirt and a pale blue strapless top. Some of the guys were in dinner suits with blue bow ties. We went to a club called Digby's in Leeds and somehow Terry managed to get me some members of the electronic dance band Bomb the Bass to come along and they got up and sang. We all got smashed.

It felt weird to be leaving Leeds after so many years there. I really felt as if it was home, and every now and then I'd feel a tremor of panic at the thought of starting again somewhere new.

Nick, the DJ at Confettis, and one of my best friends, wanted to know if I was having second thoughts.

'I know I'm going to miss everyone,' I said.

'Well, you've got Paul and you'll soon get to know new people.'

I wasn't so sure about that. In the space of a few months I'd worked out that Paul liked to have me to himself. It was weird considering he was such a life and soul of the party type. I thought maybe he was feeling possessive and a bit insecure because we were living in different parts of the country and not seeing as much of each other as we'd have liked. Although we were working together at events, we'd not really been out on that many dates. I knew the wise thing to do would be to slow down, but I just didn't know how to put the brakes on. Paul had well and truly swept me off my feet and there was no stopping him.

As the sale of the Leeds house progressed and we got closer to exchanging contracts on the one in Leicester it struck me there was a side of him that was just for me that most other people never got to see. I put it down to stress. We were both keen to get moved in together and make a fresh start. A few times I'd questioned whether I was being too hasty and he had gone out of his way to reassure me. Everybody said that moving house was one of the most stressful things you could ever go through, so no wonder he was getting a bit ratty.

'I love you, Ange. You mean the world to me. We're both stressed out, that's all,' he said.

I believed him.

39

Paul bundled me up the stairs and into the spare room. My hair was in my eyes and I stumbled, banging my hip against the wall. He shoved me onto the bed.

I glared up at him. 'What the hell do you think you're doing?'

He stood in the doorway, breathing hard, furious. 'I told you I don't want you going behind my back.'

'I was only going to phone Holly.'

'Why – so you can slag me off?'

I gasped. 'What are you saying – I can't speak to my friends any more?'

This is how it was. We'd only been in Leicester a few weeks and I could feel a noose tightening around my neck. Paul telling me what I could and couldn't do, and going off the deep end if I so much as made a phone call he didn't know about. He didn't like what I wore, didn't want me going out without him, and he definitely didn't want me keeping in touch with my friends in Leeds. I knew I had made a huge mistake but I was in so deep I didn't know what to do about it.

On the day we'd got the keys to the new house he had closed the front door behind us, grabbed me by the throat and flung me against the wall. 'You're mine now,' he said.

I had twisted free, tears running down my face, wondering what on earth I'd done putting every penny I had into a mortgage with him. I felt completely trapped. Later, he told me he was sorry, that things had been getting on top of him and he loved me so much it made him do crazy, desperate things. None of it made any sense and I wished I had listened to my mum. Now, though, it felt too late. I was working with him, up to my eyes in a joint mortgage, and too embarrassed to tell anyone what was going on. We settled into a pattern where everything was fine for a while and Paul seemed his old loving and attentive self, followed by a flare-up. Always, when something went wrong, it was my fault, or so he said, anyway. I'd get ready to go out, spend ages making myself look nice, and he would take one look at my dress and say it was too short or too low cut – that it made me look like a hooker. I had some lovely clothes but, according to him, none of them were suitable. All of a sudden I was too old to be wearing strappy little dresses any more. I looked ridiculous. When we were working, staging events, he was his usual self, charming the clients and cracking them up with his sense of humour. Everywhere we went, people said how hilarious he was, what a great guy he was, and how lucky I was to have him. It made me wonder what it was about me that brought out the worst in him. In no time at all my confidence was shattered.

We'd only been in the house a few weeks when his ex-girlfriend turned up on the doorstep. Paul went outside and shut the door behind him, so I couldn't make out what they were saying, just odd little snatches of conversation. I strained to hear, picking up snippets as the woman raised her voice, saying she was still paying for something she'd bought him, that he owed her money and she wanted him to pay up. Through the front window I could see Paul holding up his hands as if to say there was nothing he could do and in the end she went away. It was obvious she was angry and upset. He wouldn't tell me what it was about, saying she was bitter and hysterical and couldn't stand seeing him happy with someone else.

After he'd shoved me into the spare room he turned and stomped off, slamming the door behind him. I sat on the bed and buried my face in my hands, wishing I was back in Leeds with Holly, working with the Confettis crowd, having a laugh. I wished I'd never set eyes on Paul. I heard him outside the door fiddling with the handle. I got up and tried to open the door. Nothing happened. I banged on the door. 'Paul! What's going on?'

'What am I supposed to do if I can't trust you, Ange, can't even turn my back for five minutes and you're on the phone moaning to that Leeds lot?'

He was wrong about that. No one knew what was going on. I hadn't said a word. My friends thought I'd landed on my feet with a fantastic job and a man who worshipped me. I didn't know how to tell them it was nothing like that. I was too ashamed.

I rattled the handle again. It was no good, I was locked in. I stared at the door and hammered and yelled. 'Paul, for crying out loud – *open the door*!' Silence. 'Paul, will you just let me out!' I pressed my ear against the door. Nothing. He had gone back downstairs.

He left me there for hours, letting me out before he went to bed. By then I was curled up on the spare bed, exhausted from shouting and crying. 'Ange, I'm sorry, but you just wind me up. Everything was going all right and then you go and spoil it. You're here with me now, not in Leeds, and we're trying to make a fresh start. I thought that's what you wanted.' His face was sad, puzzled. 'I mean, why can't you just forget about Leeds and make a go of things here?'

I got up. 'You locked me in.'

'It's like the second I turn my back you're on the phone to someone.' It wasn't true. I hardly spoke to anyone any more. He said, 'You make me feel like I'm not enough, like you're about to run off.' He took a step closer. 'I love you so much. You're all I want. I can't stand the idea of losing you.'

'You'll drive me away at this rate.'

'I'd never do that.'

A few months after moving to Leicester the events coming through from Jeremy Taylor started to dry up. The fact Paul and I were working and living together hadn't gone down well. We decided to set up our own company and I took out a loan to help get us off the ground. I'd seen some premises not far from us that would be perfect for a model agency and started doing them up. Things remained rocky between me and Paul. The way his moods swung from one extreme to the other meant I never knew what was coming next. He was either all over me or lashing out. Most of the time I didn't want him anywhere near me, but I still felt there was no one I could tell. I felt awful, stupid for being taken in. Paul had set out to sweep me off my feet and I had let him. Being bombarded with love and attention and gifts had been such a nice feeling it had made me blind to what he was really like. The signs had been there all right – my mum had known – but I had not taken them seriously. The fact I was now in such a mess, living in a city where I knew nobody, with all my money tied up with his, was my own doing. It made me feel sick and humiliated. How could I ever tell anyone what I'd got myself into?

Most of the time I walked on eggshells around him, thinking if only I tried harder things would get better, not that it seemed to make any difference. Outside, with other people, Paul was charismatic and good company, just like he'd been when I first met him. Behind closed doors, he picked on me for the smallest, most petty things. One day, not quite managing to line up the tins in the kitchen cupboard the way he liked them with all the labels facing the front, had sparked a vicious row.

Increasingly, I felt useless, that I couldn't do anything right. Not so long ago I had been entering beauty pageants and taking charge of events at one of the biggest clubs in Leeds. Now, when I looked in the mirror I saw a shadow of the person I used to be. Paul had told me so many times I was old and past it that I believed him. I didn't feel confident or attractive any more. It didn't matter how much effort I made getting ready, trying to look my best, he would find fault: I was too old to wear my hair like that; the dress I'd put on made me look cheap. I had heard it all so many times I believed it.

40

I stood in the spare room in the dark staring out of the window. The door was locked as usual. Downstairs, the television blared away. It would be hours before Paul let me out. I eased open the window and thought about climbing onto the sill and jumping. There was nothing to grab onto outside. I looked down. What if I hurt myself, broke my ankle or something, and couldn't get away? He would find me and drag me back inside and it would make things worse.

I went and lay on the bed, completely drained, wondering how much more of this I could take. It was as if everything in my head was jumbled up and however hard I tried I couldn't make sense of it. I didn't seem able to think straight any more. The more I thought about it, the more I struggled to see a way out. I was in a long, dark tunnel, and there wasn't even a glimmer of light at the end. If I told my friends in Leeds I was being held prisoner in my own home, what would they think? It was no good. No one would believe I could have got myself into such an almighty mess, and the last thing I wanted was for anybody to know what was going on, anyway.

If only I could close my eyes and sleep and never wake up, that would be the best thing. I got under the cover and buried my face in the pillow. I didn't want to go on, not like this. I felt broken, worthless, good for nothing. I couldn't see the point. Paul kept saying he loved me and wanted to be with me and in the next breath told me I was rubbish and beat me. I pulled the covers over my head. It was nice hidden away in the dark. Maybe I didn't have to carry on. I could do something about it, find a way out, swallow painkillers or cut my wrists, end it all.

I wanted to die.

41

It was coming up to Christmas, 1990, and we were getting ready to go out. I put on a fitted red dress with a slash neck, little cap sleeves and a hemline that ended just above my knee. It looked nice and festive and at the same time I was pretty much covered up. When I came downstairs Paul took one look and told me to get changed.

'You look like you're about to go and stand on some street corner.'

I could feel the tears coming. I had made a huge effort, picked out a dress that wasn't revealing, one I was sure he couldn't object to. Nothing I ever did was right. 'What's wrong with it?'

'It's too tight for a start. And it's cheap-looking. It makes you look like a tart.'

By the time we set off, hardly speaking, me in a plain black dress, we were running late.

For the last few months I'd been busy doing up the premises I'd found nearby, getting ready to open a model agency. I'd had a catwalk built that ran the length of the building and the whole place was being painted in black, grey and white. Paul and I had got quite friendly with the bloke doing the work, Graham, and his wife, Sarah. We had arranged to meet them at a club in town.

When we got there Paul was on good form, nothing to show that barely an hour before he'd practically dragged me back upstairs and ripped my dress off my back. When he went to the bar, Sarah leaned forward and touched my arm.

'He's great, isn't he? I bet you have a right laugh at home.'

I managed a weak smile. 'Well, he's not like this all the time . . .'

'He's hysterical, proper live wire. Never a dull moment with Paul around.'

'No.'

She nodded at my glass of orange. 'Aren't you drinking, then?'

'I'm driving.'

She grinned. 'You should have got a cab, then you could've really let your hair down.'

There was another reason I wasn't drinking. I thought I might be pregnant. A few weeks before, Paul had raped me. We'd had yet another fight because I'd wanted to go round the shops on my own. That night, even though I didn't want him anywhere near me, he had pushed me onto the bed and got on top of me. I kicked and fought and screamed but he was too strong. Afterwards, I felt sick and went to sleep in the spare room. All those times he'd locked me in there and left me for hours on end and now he came after me and dragged me back into his bed. All night, I had lain awake, almost falling out of the bed, I was so desperate not even to brush against him as he slept. I thought about sneaking off and going downstairs, getting one of those scarily sharp knives we'd bought out of the block in the kitchen and putting an end to things, killing myself. Or killing him.

Now, my period was late. When I told him he was ecstatic. 'Ange, that's brilliant.' The idea I was carrying his child filled me with dread because I knew that if I had his baby I would never get away.

Sarah gave me a nudge. She was laughing and pointing. I swung round and there was Paul up on a podium, miming to a Tom Jones song, tie off, undoing his shirt. Dozens of screaming girls grabbed at him as he gyrated and stripped off. I wanted to be sick. The Paul I knew was a violent bully, yet to the rest of the world he was this madcap entertainer, always acting the fool and making people laugh. Opposite me, Sarah and Graham were in stitches. I grabbed my bag, got up and left. Just as I stepped outside Paul grabbed me from behind. His shirt was back on, undone, flapping open. He hung onto my wrist. 'Where are you going?'

'Home. You make me sick, treating me like shit then doing your Mr Nice Guy act as soon as we're out. I've had enough.' I tried to shake him off but he kept hold of me.

'Come back inside. You're making a scene.'

'I'm making a scene? You can talk.' I fished about in my bag for the car keys. 'I'm going home. Do what you want.'

I got into the car. Paul was glaring at me. He climbed into the passenger seat. 'You can't just let me have a good time, can you?' he whined.

'Oh get lost. Do what the hell you like. I'm not asking you to come with me. I couldn't care less what you do.'

Quick as a flash, his hands were round my throat. 'Don't speak to me like that, you little bitch.'

I pushed him but he kept pressing until I couldn't get my breath. He would kill me, I knew it. He tightened his grip. 'You always have to spoil things, don't you? You can't stand to see me having a good time.'

I couldn't speak, couldn't breathe. A couple with their arms round each other were walking towards us. I thrashed about, frantic, banging on the window, trying to get their attention. For one horrible moment I thought they were going to go straight past, but they stopped and the guy tapped on the passenger window. Paul looked up and let go. I put my hand to my throat and gulped in air. Paul wound down the window.

'Everything all right?'

Paul said, 'We're fine, mate, nothing to worry about.'

The guy looked at me. His girlfriend was frowning. I nodded. 'Yeah, thanks, I'm okay.'

Paul gave them a smile and reached for my hand. He squeezed it. 'Sorry, Ange,' he said. 'Let's just go home.'

In the car, Paul was calm, saying he hadn't meant to lose it like that, it was me, winding him up, and why couldn't I just get in the spirit of things like everyone else? I kept my eyes on the road.

'I've had enough, Paul, I mean it. I don't want to do this any more. It's like living with two different people, one that's all charming and funny and one that's a bloody monster. That's the one I have to put up with and I'm sick of it.'

He didn't say anything.

'I'm not happy and I can't believe you are. I get all dressed up and you just rip me to shreds. It's like you don't have a single nice thing to say to me any more.' I glanced at him. He was staring straight ahead. 'I mean, what are we even doing together?'

I thought about the joint mortgage and all the loans and felt depressed. I had been with Paul for more than a year, telling myself I'd put too much into the relationship to leave, that I had to make a go of it. I kept imagining what people would think if I walked away and lost everything. They would have me down as a complete idiot. I had been such a fool, jumped in much too fast, and now I had no idea how to get away. I gripped the steering wheel.

At home, I parked and we went in. As soon as we were inside Paul started hitting me. He knocked me down and kicked me in the stomach. I curled into a ball as he grunted and laid into me and it flashed through my head how pleased he had been when I told him I might be pregnant. Now here he was kicking me in the belly. I crawled away and he stamped on my back. The pain was so bad I thought I'd pass out. I dragged myself into the living room. Paul came after me and got hold of me by the hair, jerked my head back and slapped my face. I tasted blood. I was sobbing but I kicked out and he stopped for a second. Then I was on my feet, facing him, wiping my hand across my bloody mouth, looking for something to hurt him with. He moved towards me, his face flushed, looking at me as if I was disgusting.

'Look at the state of you,' he started to say, but I wasn't in the mood to listen any more. I was demented, raging, adrenaline in overdrive as I wrenched the television off its stand, staggered a few steps, and hurled it at him. He stumbled backwards, arms flailing, grabbing at the curtains, pulling the pole down, the TV smashing against the wall, right where he'd been standing a second or two before. He reeled, still holding the curtain, no longer disgust in his eyes now, something else. Fear, maybe. 'You mad bitch. Look what you've done.'

I was raving, screaming, making a terrible sound, scanning the room for something else to chuck at him. I would fight to the death if I had to. I was making such an awful noise, it was only a matter of time before one of the neighbours called the police.

Paul, utterly panic-stricken, put up his hands in surrender. 'Okay, okay, calm down. Christ, Ange, look at the mess.'

I kept on, screaming, yelling at him. 'Don't come near me, don't touch me, keep away.'

For months he had been pushing me and pushing me and now he had managed to tip me over the edge; he hadn't a clue what to do.

He kept his hands in the air. 'Ssh, look I'm sorry, all right? Take it easy.'

My heart thumped. I looked round the room, taking in the wreckage, the smashed TV, not sure where I'd got the strength to lift the thing.

'Look, have a bath or something,' Paul was saying. 'I'll clear up.'

I went upstairs and put my night things on. When I looked in the mirror I hardly recognized myself. My face was red and puffy, streaked with tears, mascara and blood from my split lip. In the morning it would look worse and I'd have bruises all over. The morning. I stared at myself, not able to think that far ahead. A rush of panic went through me. I couldn't stay here. Anything could happen. Now the adrenaline was wearing off I was shaking and crying, terrified of what Paul would do when he came upstairs. I crept onto the landing. The door to the living room was open. I would have to be quick. I ran down the stairs, out into the street in my dressing gown and slippers, and took off along the main road. I didn't know where I was going, just that I had to keep running. As I ran, Paul drew level in the car and crawled along beside me. I kept going.

'Ange, come on, what do you think you're doing? Get in the car.'

I ran as fast as I could, struggling to keep my slippers on.

'Ange, get in the car.'

I had already come a long way. It was two miles from our house to the roundabout at the bottom of the road and I was almost there.

I said, 'I'm not getting in with you.'

'Please. Come on.'

The roundabout was in front of me. I stopped. Where now? The car engine idled next to me. Paul said, 'Ange, let me take you home.'

'I'm not going back with you.'

'Where else can you go?'

I stood with my arms wrapped round my middle. It was cold and I was shivering. I stared at the road in front of me. Where did I think I was going in my night clothes? My bare feet in my flimsy slippers felt like blocks of ice.

'I'm not going in the house with you,' I said. I still thought he might kill me. 'Call your parents – get your dad to come.'

Paul fumbled for his mobile phone, not daring to take his eyes off me. 'Okay, I'll call them now.'

I waited while he told his dad there'd been some trouble and asked him to drive over, meet us outside the house. Reassured, I finally got in the car and we went home.

It was around 3 a.m. when his dad drove up in his works van. Paul wanted the three of us to go inside, but I wouldn't. I was terrified of getting stuck there alone with Paul. Once his dad had gone in and seen the state of the front room, with everything trashed, he came out and told me to get in the van. 'You can stay with us, Angela,' he said.

Paul turned on him. 'She's not going anywhere.'

His dad unlocked the passenger door. 'Get in the van, Angela.'

Paul swung a punch at him. His dad was tall and well-built, but he was practically a pensioner and almost went over as Paul lashed out and grappled with him, trying to get him on the ground. I sat in my dressing gown shaking from head to toe as my boyfriend wrestled with his father on the front lawn of my dream house. None of it seemed real any more.

42

When we got back Paul's mum, Brenda, was up, bustling about in the kitchen in her night clothes. She took
one look at me and the colour drained from her face.
Her eyes were shiny. 'Oh Angela, come on, I'll make
you some tea.'

I saw the look that passed between her and her
husband and it dawned on me that they'd been through
this before. Both of them looked grey, their faces lined
and ground down with worry. I watched Brenda pour
boiling water into the teapot. She was tiny, like my mum
and, in the early hours, more frail-looking and elderly
somehow than she normally seemed. Her grey curls,
usually neat, not a hair out of place, were flattened from
being in bed and there was a deep crease-line down one
side of her face. Her whole body sagged, as if there
wasn't much holding her up. No one said anything for a
minute or so.

'What on earth's been going on, Jack?' she said, eventually, not that she needed to ask. It was obvious her son
had beaten me up.

My voice was a whisper. 'It's not the first time he's done
this, is it?'

She looked away. 'I know he thinks the world of you. I
never thought . . .'

Jack took off his glasses and rubbed his eyes. 'He

even took a swing at me, Brenda.' He shook his head. 'We know he's possessive, like, but he always seemed happy with you. We thought it was all going fine, didn't we, love?'

She nodded.

'Oh, he's happy enough in front of everyone else,' I said. 'It's just when it's me and him there's trouble.' The hot tea stung my lip and I blinked, feeling tears well up. 'He kicked me round the floor like a dog tonight.' Tears ran down my face. 'I thought he was going to kill me.'

'No, Angela,' Brenda said, 'I'm sure he—'

I cut in. 'I was so scared I was like some kind of raving lunatic.' A sob escaped. 'I threw the telly at him.' Brenda shot a look at Jack. I wiped at my eyes. 'You've not seen him. He doesn't care what he does. I can't stand it.'

She put a hand on my arm. 'You need to get some sleep.' She hesitated. 'See how you feel in the morning.'

I shook my head. I knew how I'd feel in the morning.

'Every relationship goes through its ups and downs,' Jack said.

'I don't suppose you two try and kill each other, do you?'

He placed his hands flat on the table. 'You've got a lovely house, Angela. You must have been all right to start with or you'd never have bought a place together.'

Were we? I wasn't sure any more. I had fallen for the public face of Paul the charmer, and been so bowled over by him that was all I'd seen. He had made me feel amazing, so completely loved it had been overwhelming. How much of it had been real was anybody's guess.

'Get some sleep,' Brenda said. 'Tomorrow, let's see what you want to do.'

'I'm not going back – I'm scared of him.'

The next day Paul came round with flowers, full of apologies. He cried and said he loved me, it was his fault, and he never meant to let rip like that. When I'd walked out of the club he was scared I was leaving him, and then I'd said all that stuff in the car about having had enough. He couldn't bear it if he lost me. He pleaded with me to come back. We could put it behind us, he said. His parents sat with us, chipping in, saying it didn't matter what happened or how upset he was he couldn't lose his temper like that again, not ever. My face was a mess, swollen and bruised, an ugly gash in my lip. If I'd had any sense I'd have called the police, but I wasn't thinking straight, nowhere near by then, and it never even crossed my mind to report him. His parents didn't suggest it either. I didn't say much at all, just sat like a zombie while Paul went on and on about how he couldn't live without me and promised he would never ever lay a finger on me again. When he tried to hold my hand I sprung back as if I'd been scalded and he nodded and said he didn't blame me for feeling like that.

'We can start again, wipe the slate clean,' he said.

Paul spoke a lot about clean slates, fresh starts.

I said, 'I don't trust you, not any more.'

'I know, I know, and I'll make it up to you, Ange – just give me another chance.'

A clean slate. Another chance. It was all horribly familiar.

'I don't know.'

'Just think about it,' he said, giving me one of his best smiles. 'Please.'

I got Jack to take me back a couple of days later. I wasn't planning on staying long, not that I'd said so. Paul was at the front door, beaming. I went straight into the living room, where the curtains were back up and the mess had gone. A dent on the wall marked the spot where the TV had hit it. Paul smiled and rubbed his hands together. 'Ange, it's going to be great, I promise.'

I gave him a look that let him know I still was nowhere near convinced. 'Don't you have to go to work?'

'We'll talk tonight, maybe go out – have a meal or something.'

I stood at the front window watching as he drove away. Jack, in his works van, followed. Then I got on the phone to the removals guy I'd spoken to the day before and told him to give me an hour to pack.

I was going home to Grimsby.

43

Mum and Dad had moved out of the family home in Brereton Avenue and into a tiny terraced place in Grimsby. It was fine for them and my little sister Anna, who was eleven years old, but space was tight with all my furniture piled up in the hallway. They said I could stay as long as I wanted. I didn't tell them exactly what had gone on with Paul, just that we'd had a fight. I was still too ashamed to say how bad things had got or that he'd been knocking me about for ages.

From the moment Paul had got home from work and found me gone he had been calling. In the end, I switched off my mobile phone. I didn't want to speak to him. I had done a pregnancy test and it was positive. My head was in a complete spin. I had only been in Grimsby a few days when he turned up on the doorstep. I hid in my room with the door open a crack as Dad stood at the front door talking to him. All I could hear were hushed voices but I couldn't make out what was being said. I just kept thinking: Don't let him in. Whatever you do, don't let him in.

The sight of Paul, white-faced, in tears, begging to see me, got to my dad and in the end he let him in.

'He's in a right state, Angela,' Dad said. 'He just wants to talk to you.'

I shook my head. 'Dad, it's no good, you don't know what he's like.'

'Just have a word.'

'I don't want to see him.'

'He's come all this way now. I can't just send him away.'

I stood at the end of the bed with my arms folded.

'You need to sort out what you're doing with the house, anyway.'

Dad made cups of tea while Paul begged for another chance. *One last chance.* He grovelled and pleaded. According to him, we had so much going for us we couldn't just throw it all away. He knew he had to keep his temper in check and stop going off the deep end and he would, he promised. He was sorry, really sorry about what he'd done. He wanted to make it up to me. He loved me so much. I was all he wanted.

I said, 'I'm pregnant.'

His face changed, the tortured look replaced by a tentative smile. 'Really?'

'I've done a test.'

'Ange, that's great news. We'll start again, make things right this time, I promise.' He grinned. 'We're having a baby.'

I shook my head. 'We're not. I'm not having it.'

The smile slipped. 'What? We can put things right. Clean slate.'

Another clean slate. 'You're so jealous, Paul, so possessive all the time. Look how you are with me – how could I bring a baby into that?'

'It won't be like that.'

'No. I can't do it. I'm not doing it.' I'd made up my mind. There was no way I'd bring a baby into all this misery. It wasn't fair. Despite all his declarations of love, Paul had proved himself a violent bully to me. Who was to say he'd be any different with his child? I couldn't take the chance.

Mum didn't want me to go back to Leicester. She was in bed with a migraine when I went to tell her I was leaving. I sat on the edge of the bed with her in the dark. 'Don't go back, Angela,' she said. 'He'll only do it again.'

She was getting lots of migraines and some days she looked really poorly. I don't suppose it helped knowing my life was in crisis. I knew I was welcome to stay at home as long as I wanted but I could see there wasn't room for me long term. It was a tiny house to start with and now, with all my stuff piled up downstairs, it had started to look like a junk shop. You could hardly get along the hall for all the clutter. Plus, I didn't want Paul turning up all the time, making scenes, dragging my parents into our problems. It wasn't fair. There was my sister Anna to think about as well. I didn't want any of this to impact on her. One way or another, I needed to sort things out properly and that meant making some tough decisions.

I had no money, was up to my eyes in debt, and the only asset I had was the house in Leicester. I couldn't afford to just walk away from it, or so I thought. Walking away didn't feel like an option. Go where? Do what? After everything that had been going on with Paul I wasn't the same fearless girl who would turn up in a new city with all her belongings in a couple of bin liners. I was fragile and afraid, completely lacking in confidence. Paul had pulled me to bits so many times I felt as old and useless as he kept telling me I was. In my head – something I didn't dare say to Mum and Dad – there was a nagging doubt that I was the reason it had all gone wrong. Everybody else loved Paul. Out and about, he was full of life, a natural entertainer – so why wasn't he like that when it was just him and me? I almost sent myself mad trying to work out what it was about me that turned this great guy into a vicious bully. In my more sane moments I knew, of course, that it was nothing to do with me, but those sane moments were thin on the ground. The one thing that kept me going was that I was nearly ready to open the model agency. If I could just get that up and running and make a go of it, at least I'd have some financial independence and then maybe, just maybe, I could get away from him once and for all. For now, that seemed the best thing to do, the only option I could come up with. I decided to go back and give it one last go.

44

I was in the bedroom, hanging stuff up in the wardrobe when Paul came in. He sidled up behind me and put his arms round my waist. I felt my whole body tense.

'Come on, Ange, it's been ages.'

I tried to push him away. 'I don't want to, okay?'

He held onto me. 'You never want to.'

It was only a few weeks since I'd had the abortion. I had gone to a clinic in Birmingham and driven through a crowd of protestors who'd waved placards at me and shouted and banged on the side of the car. It had been horrendous. Because I didn't really know anyone in Leicester I'd asked a woman I'd only met a few times to come with me and was grateful to have her there, glad I didn't have to run the gauntlet on my own. Afterwards, I didn't want Paul anywhere near me, and for a while he kept his distance.

Now, he shoved me onto the bed. 'I'm a bloke, Ange, I can't go without for ever, you know.'

I struggled and tried to fight him off but he had me pinned down. He was going to rape me again. Panic went through me. It was like the night he'd kicked me round the floor when something inside went snap and the adrenaline kicked in. I reached up, grabbed his tie with both hands, and started to pull. His face went red and his eyes widened. There was spit on his mouth. I pulled as hard as

I could as he made odd gasping sounds. His face was a strange colour, almost blue, and his eyes bulged. It went through my mind that all I had to do was hold on and it would be over, once and for all. That's when I came to my senses. I didn't want to go to jail. I didn't want Paul to turn me into a killer. I let go and he fell backwards onto the bed, wheezing, struggling for breath, clutching at his neck. I got up and stood over him. I was trembling, in floods of tears. It was getting on for two years since I had first met Paul and he had swept me off my feet. Now I was at the end of my rope. My voice shook. 'If you ever touch me again I *will* kill you.'

This time when I left all I took were my clothes and a poxy little portable TV.

45

There was a flat above the model agency and nobody living in it, so I took the lease. I hadn't been there long when my mum and dad split up. I couldn't believe it. They had been married getting on for thirty years, and despite all their ups and downs I'd always thought they would grow old together. When I went up to Grimsby to find out what was going on Dad had already moved out and Mum was adamant she wouldn't have him back.

I met Dad at a café and was shocked at the state of him. He looked as though he hadn't slept for days. He wouldn't say what he'd done to Mum, only that he was to blame for everything, and there was no way she would take him back. He sat there, in tears, saying what a mess he'd made of everything.

It was heartbreaking seeing him in bits. I said, 'What are you going to do, Dad?'

He shrugged, helpless. 'I don't know. I've got nowhere to go.'

A thought jumped into my head. 'Come and live with me in Leicester.'

He gave me a funny look. 'What would I do there?'

'I don't know – get a job. You'd find something.' He was only fifty and he had loads of strings to his bow: manual work, driving, even a stint teaching learner drivers.

He looked a bit bewildered.

'We'd have a laugh. Plus, I'm on my own and Paul's only down the road so you'd be doing me a favour. He's not going come round shouting the odds if you're there.'

Dad gazed at me. His eyes were dull and red-rimmed. He managed a smile. 'Are you serious?'

'I'm dead serious.'

He rubbed his chin. 'Well, that's the answer, then.'

'You'll come?'

'I will.'

I loved having my dad around. I'd got the agency, Leicester Model Team, up and running and even managed to get a few local dignitaries along to the launch party. I knew it would take time to drum up business so I was offering weekend courses in modelling to bring in some money. Meanwhile, I had to do something about all the loans I'd taken out while I was with Paul. I had been so stupid. Everything was in my name. I'd even borrowed money to get his ex-girlfriend off his back. When I added it all up I was in debt to the tune of around £20,000 and had no idea how I was going to keep meeting the payments. The income I was generating through the agency wasn't nearly enough. I didn't want to let things get completely out of hand so I went to the Citizen's Advice Bureau and took all my paperwork – bank statements, credit card bills, loan agreements, the lot – with me. One of their debt advisers went through it all and came up with a plan of attack that meant I could make lower monthly payments and keep chipping away at what I owed. I was so embarrassed to have got into such a mess. I had lost everything. At the same time, I was thankful to be alive and in a position to at least start making inroads into the debts hanging over me. I knew I would never see a penny of the money I'd put into the house.

Every now and then Paul called, asking me to go back to him, and each time I told him I wanted nothing more to do with him. Somehow, I knew it would be a while before he got the message. He had never been good at taking no for an answer.

One morning, I was in the agency going through some head shots, and a photographer I was working with, Terry Hanson, who'd become a good friend, was behind reception when the door opened and Paul, flanked by two big blokes, breezed in. All three were carrying baseball bats and wearing matching, ill-fitting shell suits. I felt my heart rate start to go up. Terry took one look at the baseball bats and said, 'Shall I call the police?'

Paul gave me a nasty smile. 'This is the bitch I was telling you about,' he said to the guys standing on either side of him. 'She needs to be taught a lesson.' He glanced round the room. 'You've got this place looking nice, Ange. Shame to mess it up.'

I stared at him. No way was I going to let him ruin everything I had worked so hard for, not just as I was starting to get back on my feet. Behind me, Terry, said, 'Shall I—'

I took a step closer to Paul and screamed at the top of my voice. '*Get out!* Get off my premises NOW or I'm calling the police. All of you – *GET OUT!*'

I could feel my heart racing. Paul put up a hand. 'Come on, lads, let's get out. I told you she's a nutter.'

As soon as they'd gone I called the police.

Afterwards, everything went quiet. I didn't hear from Paul, I didn't see him, and with my dad around I felt safe.

In the middle of all the trouble with Paul and my parents splitting up, my nana got ill with stomach cancer. She'd had a pretty tough life, bringing up four children, working in the Findus factory, losing her grandson to cot death, then my granddad had contracted pneumonia and died. In the ten years since his death she had lived life to the full, going abroad on holiday, dancing, making the most of every moment. She had even joined a dance troupe and tapped her way across the Humber Bridge for charity, ending up in fishnets and a leotard on Cilla Black's *Surprise, Surprise* show. In 1983, on holiday in Scarborough, I'd won a beauty contest at the Grand Hotel and she had won the glamorous grandmother contest. She had looked lovely that night with her hair in soft curls and wearing a smart cocktail dress that showed off her figure. I had watched her on stage, sparkling, full of life, thinking how much my mum looked like her.

Every time I went to visit her after she got ill, she had shrunk a bit more. She seemed to be wasting away, disappearing in front of us, and there was nothing anyone could do to save her. By the time cancer had been diagnosed, it was already inoperable. It only seemed five minutes since she'd been living it up on holiday in Malaga and I couldn't imagine how awful it was for Mum seeing her go downhill so fast, fading away, literally, until she was just skin and bone, a tiny size four, all in the space of a few months. When she died the crematorium was filled with flowers, absolutely overflowing with wreaths and bouquets from family and friends. No one had ever seen anything like it.

It was only when Mum was going through her stuff that she found a scrapbook under the bed filled with newspaper cuttings from the beauty pageants I'd won. I think she had been as surprised as anyone when her painfully shy sixteen-year-old granddaughter had entered the Miss Yorkshire TV pageant and got herself in the *Grimsby Evening Telegraph*. She had never said much, beyond expressing amazement that I had it in me to parade along a catwalk in a swimsuit. 'Our Angela,' she used to say, mystified. 'Who'd have thought it?'

I'd never known what she really thought or even if she approved, but as I leafed through the scrapbook and saw the pictures of me as Miss Cleethorpes, Miss Leeds Metro, Miss Lovely Legs, Miss Southport English Rose, in among stories about me modelling in Dubai, working for Rolls Royce, posing with John Harvey Jones, the Chairman of ICI, I knew she must have been ever so proud.

46

On Christmas Eve, 1991, one of my models, Amanda Forbes, persuaded me to have a night out at Crystals, a club in town. I'd not done anything socially for nearly a year and the only party I'd been to was the one to launch the agency. It suited me staying in, but Amanda was adamant. 'It'll do you good, Ange – what you going to do otherwise? Watch telly on your own?'

I quite liked watching telly on my own but I didn't want to say so. Twenty-seven seemed a bit young to have turned into a complete couch potato. Finally, after much persuading, I gave in and told Amanda I'd go.

Dad had gone to the pub and I was getting ready when the doorbell went. I opened up to find Paul standing there. I jumped and tried to slam the door shut but he stuck his foot in the gap.

'You'd better go or I'll call the police.'

He looked me up and down. 'You're all dressed up – are you going out?'

'None of your business.'

'Ange, I still love you.'

'For God's sake, Paul, drop it, will you? It's hardly five minutes since you wanted to trash my business.' I glared at him. 'You looked ridiculous by the way, you and your heavies in your matching shell suits.'

'I wasn't going to do anything.'

'Course you weren't.'

'Where are you going – out with some bloke?'

'I've told you, it's nothing to do with you. Now go away.'

He kept his foot in the door. 'I miss you. I want you back. Can't we give it another go?'

I looked at him, not believing what I was hearing. 'Are you mad? How many times do I have to tell you?' I shoved at the door and he shifted his foot an inch or two. 'I'm calling the police and Dad's due back any second, so you'd better get going. Just leave me alone.' I managed to shut the door and slide the bolt. My hands were shaking. It was ridiculous. I was never going to get rid of him at this rate.

I phoned Amanda. 'Sorry, I've got this lunatic ex who's turned up and I can't get out.'

'I'll get you a cab.'

'It's not worth it. I know what he's like and he'll only cause trouble.'

'What, so you're going let him keep you prisoner in your own home?'

That rang a horrible bell.

She said, 'Come on, Ange, I'll get a cab to pick you up in half an hour. Don't let some nutcase get to you – get out and enjoy yourself.'

We were in the VIP room of the club when a good-looking guy with dark hair and twinkly brown eyes came over and started chatting, telling us jokes, and making us laugh. His name was John and he had a glass business in Leicester. The last thing I wanted was any male attention but he was so funny and easy going I started to relax. When he asked if he could see me again I wasn't sure. He seemed like a nice enough guy but so had Paul. For so long I had taken people at face value and now I wasn't sure I could any more. I told him I wasn't really looking for a relationship and he just shrugged and smiled. 'You can still go out, can't you?'

I thought about what Amanda had said earlier about Paul keeping me a prisoner and realized he still could – if I let him. I could stay in night after night and never get involved with anyone again, or I could take my chances. It was up to me. I agreed to meet John a couple of days later.

He didn't drive so I arranged to pick him up at the station in Leicester. He'd only just got into the car when I checked my mirror and spotted Paul in a van behind me. I knew he must have been following me.

I felt a familiar jolt of panic. 'John, I just need to tell you something. My ex is mental and he's in the van behind us.'

John shrugged. He didn't look in the least bit fazed. 'Okay, let's just ignore him.'

At the first red light I stopped at Paul jumped out of the van, leaving the driver's door wide open. I snapped down the locks as he ran towards the car, tugging at the handle, banging on the window. John wasn't looking so relaxed any more. 'See what you mean,' he said.

The lights changed and I drove on. Paul stuck like glue. We stopped again and he strode round to the front of the car, leaning forward, jabbing a finger first at me, then at John. 'You're going to die,' he yelled. 'He's going to die!'

The traffic started to move and he ran back to the van. Every time I had to stop he pulled some stunt or other, drawing up alongside and hurling abuse or swerving in front of me. I had visions of him ploughing into us at speed. My hair was sticking to the back of my neck and my hands felt clammy. I was absolutely terrified.

'I'm going have to go the police station,' I said. 'He's quite capable of killing us.'

I drove to Church Street station and John ran inside for help as Paul drew up next to me and wound down his window. 'I'll kill you, you bitch,' he screamed. 'I'll kill you!' Then he put his foot down and sped off.

Over the next couple of hours I gave a statement, saying I was in fear for my life. I told the police Paul had been violent in the past, although I didn't go into detail. The whole time, John sat with me. It wasn't what you'd call the perfect first date. Later, he said he had been out with a girl not long before and they'd been chased by her mad ex, too. 'I'm beginning to think it's me,' he said, making a joke, letting me know it was okay, that he wasn't judging me. I thought he'd never want to see me again. I certainly didn't feel ready to get involved with anyone. It was far too soon for that. John didn't mind. We started going out, just as friends, and I got a restraining order against Paul. If he came anywhere near me he would be locked up. I didn't hear another word from him. At last, he seemed to understand it was over and no amount of threats or begging for another chance would make the slightest bit of difference.

47

I'd been seeing John for a few months when he asked me to go on holiday with him. He was thinking of a week in Florida followed by a week in the Bahamas. It sounded fantastic but I was nervous. After everything that had happened with Paul, I had a huge issue with trust. Even though I liked John and he was fun to be with I had my guard up. I definitely wasn't ready to sleep with him. I didn't know if I ever would be. He didn't make a big deal out of it, just said it would do us the world of good to get away and soak up some sunshine and it would be his treat. That threw me for a start. When I had been with Paul we had gone on holiday to Thailand but I had picked up the tab. The whole trip had been dismal, with us arguing about me wearing little summer skirts and tops. Even though it was absolutely roasting, Paul insisted I cover up. When I looked back at the photos I couldn't believe I'd worn those drab, shapeless clothes.

I spoke to my sister Becky, and told her I was wary about going away with John. If it all went wrong I'd be thousands of miles from home. 'I'm worried something will happen and I won't be able to get back,' I said.

'Take a credit card, just so you know you could get on a flight if you had to,' Becky said. She waited a second. 'I'm sure you'll be okay, you know. He seems like a really nice guy. I mean, he could have run a mile after all that business with Paul to start with and he didn't.'

She was right. John had stuck around when he could easily have legged it. He was laid back and funny and kind – and I didn't feel any pressure to take things further unless I wanted to.

We stayed in a lovely hotel on International Drive, in Orlando. I loved Florida, the way everything seemed larger than life, even the portions every time we sat down to eat. At Disney World we went on every ride we could, including something called the Tower of Terror that was like a spooky old hotel with a lift that dropped like a stone. It frightened the life out of me. We even queued up with all the kids to go on the ET ride. We went to SeaWorld where watching the dolphins perform brought a lump to my throat. It was magical. In between, we sunbathed by the pool at the hotel, where on the first day I'd really put my foot in it by taking my bikini top off. It caused quite a stir. I had no idea you couldn't sunbathe topless in the States and was absolutely mortified when one of the hotel staff rushed up to tell me. On our last night we went for an Indian meal at a restaurant not far from the hotel, and as I ate my chicken curry I thought it didn't taste right. The next day on the flight to the Bahamas I started to feel poorly. I just made it to the loo on the plane before being violently sick. Throughout the flight I was throwing up and in between bouts of sickness I was doubled up with stomach cramps and diarrhoea. I didn't need a doctor to tell me the dodgy chicken from the night before had given me food poisoning. By the time we landed I felt like death.

John had booked us into a fabulous hotel right on the beach. It was one of those idyllic places with hammocks strung between palm trees and hardly a soul in sight. The sun blazed down and the sea was the most amazing colour, turquoise near the shore and a deep, brilliant blue further out. It was like someone had drawn a line between the two blocks of colour. It was pristine, the nicest beach I'd ever seen, and I was so ill all I wanted to do was crawl into bed.

For the next three days I stayed in the room, feeling awful. I couldn't keep a thing down. The hotel doctor came and I took all kinds of medicine. Nothing made the slightest bit of difference. John was so good, keeping me company, just wanting me to feel better. I was absolutely mortified to think he was seeing me in such a bedraggled state, washed-out and hollow-eyed and with that sour smell you get when you're being constantly sick. I didn't want his entire holiday to be ruined and begged him to go out and get some air, at least do some sunbathing. 'There's no point in both of us hiding away in a darkened room,' I said, relieved when he finally agreed, reluctantly, to leave me on my own for a couple of hours.

On day four he took me to see another doctor, a huge man who sprawled in his chair, feet up on his desk, puffing on a cigar.

'I can give you something to get it out of your system,' he said, 'but you're going to feel worse before you get better.'

I looked at John. I was willing to try anything.

The doctor produced a syringe and gave me a shot of something. He was still explaining that what he'd given me would speed up the whole process of recovery when

I had a horribly familiar feeling. I was going to be sick. I ran from his surgery and locked myself in the toilet and threw up. I seemed to be in there for ages, feeling about a hundred times worse than I had at any point in the previous few days. Finally, I stopped throwing up and started to feel a bit better. That was it. I was over the worst. Whatever it was he gave me had done the trick. The next day, John and I went to the beach and had a lazy day, stretched out in the hammocks, taking dips in the sea. We had three perfect days. I was bowled over by how caring and thoughtful he had been, never complaining, just wanting me to be okay.

By the time we came home we were a proper couple.

48

The model agency was doing all right and the weekend classes were bringing in business, but I still wasn't making enough money. To get the really big bookings and lucrative campaigns you had to be in London. I had also struggled to make friends in Leicester and still didn't know many people. It had been much easier to get in with a good crowd when I'd made the move from Grimsby to Leeds, but in my new home I was starting to despair of ever finding anyone on my wavelength. Among the few close friends I had made was a girl who had turned up at the agency one day looking for modelling work. Anuapama Jaidka was bright, bubbly and very pretty with long dark hair and green eyes. The two of us clicked right away. As soon as I saw her I was convinced she had the potential to be a successful beauty queen and I worked with her for several weeks, teaching her how to walk on the catwalk, do her hair and make-up and so on. We became firm friends and our hard work paid off when, in 1991, wearing the blue dress I'd worn on the night I took the Miss Leeds Metro title, Anu won the Miss Asia UK crown. She went on to compete in Miss Asia World in New York. The two of us then formed the Asian Model Team, which ran alongside my original Leicester Model Team.

Meanwhile, I took a job at a fashion shop in St Martin's, a quaint little shopping area in Leicester. I contacted the Miss World office and managed to get the licence to organize the

Miss Leicester pageant. It was a really big thing for me and I was determined to make a success of it. The owner of the shop where I was working let me put up photos of the girls taking part and I did a big window display to try to get people interested. We got lots of entries just through passing trade. I did what I could to drum up some local press coverage as well, but the response was lukewarm. In the early nineties, it was an uphill struggle getting the media interested in covering beauty pageants. I staged the competition in a club called Jokers and it went without a hitch, with the title, and a place in Miss UK, going to a girl called Julie Gillam from Leamington Spa. I was really pleased with the way it all worked out since it was the first competition I'd done for the Miss World organization. Afterwards, though, there was a fair bit of negative press because a local girl hadn't won. I'd put so much effort into the whole thing I was upset by the backlash and phoned Eric Morley at the Miss World office to make sure it was okay to have a Miss Leicester who came from somewhere else. The last thing I wanted was to land in trouble with my first pageant.

Eric Morley was brusque and to the point.

'Miss UK is a national competition,' he said, sounding slightly exasperated. 'You can qualify anywhere.'

'Right . . .'

'Do people expect the tennis players who win Wimbledon to come from there?'

'Well, no, I . . .'

'It doesn't matter where you come from or where you qualify.'

I was probably on the phone less than a minute.

*

Being with John was good for me. After what I'd been through with Paul my faith in relationships was in tatters. I really hadn't wanted to get involved with anyone else and then John came along and reminded me that there were still kind and decent men in the world. It can't have been easy for him being with someone who found it so hard to trust anybody. The whole Paul experience had made me wary, a bit paranoid even. I was always on the alert for signs to show that John wasn't who he said he was. I told him what had happened with Paul, just dribs and drabs to start with, keeping much of it to myself. I still felt ashamed. John took everything in his stride and gave me the time and space I needed, never putting me under pressure, letting me be myself. He was easy to be around, laid-back, always up for having a good time, and he made me laugh. It was so long since I'd had any fun that he was just what I needed. And when I got ready to go out he would invariably say I looked nice instead of hurling insults at me.

I thought I had finally heard the last of Paul, but one day I was at the agency and a call came in from someone at the building society we'd had our mortgage with for the house in Leicester. The woman explained that Paul had stopped paying the mortgage for several months in the run-up to the house being repossessed and had now disappeared. Since it had been a joint mortgage, I was liable for the debts. My heart sank. I had invested all I had in the house, lost the lot, and now I might have to fork out even more. It didn't seem fair. I started to tell her exactly what had gone on between us – the bullying, the beatings, and the eventual restraining order after he chased me round town threatening to kill me. I said that after having put thousands of pounds into the property I had walked away with nothing besides a cheap little TV. I was on the phone for ages explaining how much in debt I was, telling her about all the loans I'd taken out so Paul could have a car, pay off his girlfriend, and God knows what else, and how the Citizens Advice Bureau had helped me get things straight. I told her absolutely everything. For so long I had been ashamed and gone out of my way to hide what was going on with Paul. Not any more. As I poured my heart out she kept quiet. In the end, she said now she knew where I was she'd be in touch if there was anything else. I hung up, thinking yet another debt was about to land on me but it never did. That was the last I ever heard.

As time went on, I got back some of the old me I'd thought was gone for good. I knew John had come along at exactly the right time and I thanked God for him. It was a huge step for me to live with someone else but when he moved into the flat above the agency I knew it was the right thing. For a while my dad lived there too, and at one point so did my sister Becky and her boyfriend. We had some good times, although space was very tight. It was so good for me to be with people I loved and cared about. Then I saw a house up for sale, one that had been repossessed and was a bargain at £32,000. It was in Dartford Road, not far from the centre of Leicester, and needed everything doing – damp proofing, electrics, plumbing, the lot. I'm not sure John was as keen as I was initially but it was too good an opportunity to miss. For the next few months we lived in absolute chaos while the work was being done. There were no internal doors – the previous owners had taken them – and no heating. It was absolutely freezing and we spent weeks sleeping on a mattress in the living room with our coats on. I kept the licence for Miss Leicester and took on another one for Miss Nottingham. Every now and then it would strike me I was running these glamorous events and at the same time practically living in a hovel.

I was gradually getting back on my feet financially, whittling down the debts I'd built up when I was with Paul, expanding the beauty pageant side of things to include Miss Birmingham alongside Miss Leicester and Miss Nottingham. One of the models I had on my books put me in touch with someone she knew who wanted to stage a beauty pageant at his pub in Mansfield.

John Singh was forty-something with a string of business interests in the Midlands. I agreed to set up a Miss Early Doors competition at one of his pubs and organized it as a fashion show with weekly heats and a grand final. It was a big success and boosted his midweek trade. John Singh knew I had arranged regional competitions for the Miss World organization and was keen to get involved somehow. I suggested that one way might be to sponsor the Miss UK event through another company he had, Worldwide Snooker Promotions.

I went to London to pitch the idea to the Miss World office. Other than on TV I had only seen Eric Morley once before, at a Miss England heat at a leisure centre in Doncaster, when I had been one of about a hundred girls taking part. We'd all turned up clutching our little vanity cases, carrying swimsuits and high heels; some of the girls arrived with their hair in rollers. We'd got changed and gone into a room, twelve at a time, to face the judges, who were lined up behind a long table. It was all very slickly done with Eric Morley in his dinner suit reeling off each girl's name, getting us to pose in our line up this way and that. 'Now, ladies, take a half turn to the left,' he'd said. 'Now, all the way round, backs to the judges, please – and facing the front again.' The judges, including Wilnelia Merced, the former Miss Puerto Rico who had won Miss World 1975 and subsequently married Bruce Forsyth, had scribbled on their clipboards as we'd filed out and the next batch of girls had gone in. It had been over in no time at all and I hadn't made the next stage of the heat.

A few years later, in the Miss World office in Golden Square, in my best business suit, I outlined John Singh's sponsorship proposal to Eric Morley. It was 1994 and sponsors weren't easy to come by. Eric agreed that World-wide Snooker Promotions would promote Miss UK. I ran things for John, setting up an office in Mansfield and commuting from Leicester each day. We decided to shoot a 'Snooker with Beauty' calendar featuring players like Steve Davis and Terry Griffiths paired up with Miss UK contestants in evening wear. The only hitch during the entire shoot was the day we were due to photograph Jimmy 'the Whirlwind' White with Miss Nottingham, Angie Bowness, at London's Dorchester Hotel. We were in John Singh's Rolls Royce, heading down Park Lane, Jimmy saying he felt a bit the worse for wear after a late night, and then, without any warning, deciding he didn't want to do the shoot after all. I was halfway through say-ing there was nothing to worry about when the car pulled up at a red light and he jumped out. We all stared after him, helpless, as he sprinted off in the direction of Grosvenor Square. There was nothing anybody could do, other than fix another date. That time, he did turn up. The idea was that the calendar would be promoted in a national newspaper, but for whatever reason it didn't happen and we ended up with piles of unsold merchandise.

By then, John Singh was hooked on the beauty-pageant business, and looking to spread his wings. He registered the title Miss Great Britain and decided to compete with Miss UK. He wanted me to work for him full time and run the contest. Ever since I was a little girl, I had been in awe of Miss World and, in my eyes, Eric Morley was the undisputed king of the beauty-pageant world. His competition had been running since 1951 and had that long-established, solid feel to it. Eric was such a hard worker and knew the business inside out – I couldn't help admire him. Although the idea of being in at the start of a new venture was to some degree exciting I wanted to stick with what I knew. I turned John Singh down and, instead, persuaded Eric Morley to put me on the payroll to run Miss UK for him.

49

By 1996 I was running Miss UK and at the same time planning my wedding. It was me more than John who'd pushed to get married because I'd reached a stage in my life where I wanted to feel more secure. Since moving to Leicester I'd not really felt that I had properly put down roots, not the way I had in Leeds, and I thought settling down might give me a sense of belonging. I would have loved my parents to see me married but since they weren't on good terms it made things difficult. In the end, John and I decided to get married abroad in September, just the two of us, no family or friends. Mum and Dad said they were fine with that, although I suspected Dad was secretly disappointed. We chose Hawaii, just because neither of us had ever been there and it looked like paradise, a real dream destination, and the perfect setting to exchange our vows on the beach. We arranged to go for three weeks, booked it all through a travel agent in Leicester, making sure we planned as much as we could. We wanted it to be a really memorable trip and decided to spend our first week in Oahu, Hawaii's third biggest island, then move onto Kauai for the second week, which was smaller and ideal for the actual wedding. Our last week would be in Las Vegas. It was quite an ambitious itinerary but we had plenty of time – so we thought.

I don't think I'd appreciated how far away Hawaii – a

whopping 8,000 miles from home – actually is. We flew to San Francisco and caught a connecting flight to Honolulu. We had something like half an hour to get from one plane to the next and had to run through the terminal building to make the flight. We did it by the skin of our teeth. How our luggage made it, I will never know. By the time the plane landed in Oahu we had been flying for eighteen hours and were exhausted and completely disorientated. We picked up a hire car and I drove from the airport in the south right to the northern tip of the island where, even though we had a week to go before the wedding, we'd booked the honeymoon suite in a hotel on the beach at Kahuku. By the time we got there we were both so past ourselves with tiredness that we barely took in how fabulous the room was with its view over the sea, and fell asleep with our clothes on. We didn't even bother with the complimentary bottle of champagne. I think we slept for almost a day. Hawaii is ten hours behind the UK and it took me days to get over the jet lag. Luckily, the hotel was in such a nice spot we were happy to relax and sunbathe. The only bit of sightseeing we did was a trip one day to Waikiki Beach to see where they filmed *Hawaii Five-0*.

At the hotel, we bumped into an older couple from Newcastle, Mel and Mervyn. They were proper Geordies, really lovely, and got very excited when we told them we were getting married the following week.

'Oh, that's a shame,' Mel said. 'We're in Kauai next week.'

'So are we – that's where we're getting married! Do you want to be our guests?'

They beamed at us.

'Our *only* guests,' I said. 'We're doing it on the quiet, just the two of us.'

John grinned. 'We're not ones for making a fuss.'

'No,' I said, 'apart from the limo and the champagne on the beach and the horse-drawn carriage afterwards . . . no fuss at all!'

Mel's brow furrowed. 'Oh, we can't let you get married with nobody there, pet – can we Mervyn?' He shook his head.

I was glad to think we'd have at least a couple of friendly faces to witness us exchanging our vows and wished there'd been a way for my mum and dad to be there too.

Kauai was absolutely beautiful, a tiny island where nobody was in a hurry to do anything. On the roads, the traffic tootled along at about twenty miles an hour maximum. I don't think they'd heard of speeding. We flew in from Honolulu on a small plane that gave us an amazing view of the Na Pali coast where *Jurassic Park* was filmed. Everything in sight was green and lush and completely unspoiled.

The night before the wedding we had arranged to have dinner with Mel and Mervyn, who were staying in a villa about a ten-mile drive from us. On the way, we ran out of petrol and Mervyn came to rescue us. We ended up staying the night at their place and, in keeping with eve of wedding tradition, sleeping in separate rooms on put-me-up beds. The next day, we went for petrol, rescued the car, and I went back to the hotel on my own to get ready. I didn't want John to see me until just before the ceremony.

I'd had my wedding dress made by a designer called

Carole Lee, from Newark, who I'd got to know through the Miss Nottingham pageant. She'd made a short white dress with a floaty layered handkerchief skirt and a fitted bodice. It was satin and chiffon with tiny crystals dotting the bodice and the points of the hem. Carole had made matching satin shoes and a hair clip that had a cluster of delicate little tassels studded with crystals. I started to get ready, did my make-up, and swept my hair into an up do. I'd arranged for someone to come to the room and do my nails. Outside, it was a glorious day, a slight breeze ruffling the leaves of the palm trees, sun beating down, the surface of the Pacific Ocean sparkling. Perfect for a wedding on the beach. All of sudden I wished my family was there and tears stung my eyes. I wanted my mum in a posh frock and buttonhole, fussing about, helping me into my wedding dress, and Dad giving me away. I wanted my brothers and sisters there. Alone in the hotel room, I had a little cry. It was mad. There I was, in a corner of paradise, about to be married, with tears streaming down my face. It was what John and I had said we wanted, the best thing to do, bearing in mind Mum and Dad had fallen out. Now, though, thousands of miles from home, I realized how sad I was not to have them there. Lovely as it was to tie the knot on a beach in Hawaii, I'd never pictured my wedding day with none of my family around me. I dried my eyes and repaired my make-up, not wanting John to see me in a state. The last thing I wanted was to spoil his big day.

A limo decked out with white ribbon swept us from the front of the hotel to the beach, a journey that took all of about two minutes. John and I made our vows as waves broke against the shore behind us, him in a white linen jacket, black trousers and natty bow tie, me with my satin heels sinking into the sand. We exchanged rings, gold bands of overlapping leaves that were just like miniature versions of the Hawaiian leis round our necks. After a short, simple service I was Mrs Angela Beasley. John and I got into a horse-drawn carriage and went for a ride round the nearby botanical gardens before returning to the beach to sink champagne with Mel and Mervyn. All I remember is the sun going down and the sound of the waves breaking on the beach and ruining my lovely hand-made shoes on the damp sand. Oh, and knocking back the champagne until we were all completely drunk!

From Kauai we flew to Las Vegas which, after the peace and quiet of a small, slow-paced Pacific island, was, to put it mildly, a bit of a shock to the system. Vegas is a crazy place with its bright lights, tacky wedding chapels and all-night gambling and our hotel, the Mirage, was right in the thick of things. I had never seen anything like it. Inside the lobby, running the whole length of the reception desk, was a giant aquarium with sharks swimming about in it. It was completely outrageous. Every night a full-blown pirate battle was staged outside the hotel in front of thousands of tourists. The scale of the high-rise buildings along the famous Strip and the neon and nightlife astonished me. One night we went to a club that projected massive video images all round the walls of everybody on the dance floor. One of the best things we did was see Siegfried and Roy's white-tiger show. We were right at the front and got a close-up view of the choreography, which was amazing – what looked like hundreds of dancers, all flawless, and moving in perfect sync with one another.

I don't think I was mentally prepared for how in your face Las Vegas is, and I hated being accosted every time we went out – people shoving flyers with pictures of beautiful women at us, saying John could have any girl he liked sent to our hotel room. The fact we were hand in hand, both wearing wedding rings and obviously a couple, made not the slightest bit of difference. We didn't get a minute's peace.

Neither of us had properly got over the jet lag we'd suffered right at the start of the trip and changing time zones again seemed to knock us for six. Because we'd wanted the holiday to be special we tried to pack in as much as we could, booking shows and excursions, not thinking we might be overdoing things a bit. A highlight of our final week was meant to be a flight over the Grand Canyon, but on the day we were going we overslept and woke just minutes before the tour bus was picking us up from the hotel. We ran through the lobby, past the sharks in the giant fish tank, throwing on clothes as we went, and scrambled onto the bus, unwashed, hair all over, seconds before the doors slid shut and it set off. Both of us had been looking forward to getting a bird's eye view of one of the wonders of the world but neither of us could keep our eyes open. By the time our twelve-seater plane was over the Grand Canyon the pair of us had nodded off.

We missed the whole thing.

50

In March 1998 I discovered I was pregnant. The news was
a bolt out of the blue as I'd been using a contraceptive
injection and didn't think for one second I could conceive.
Naively, I had always imagined that having a baby was
something you planned, taking into account your work
commitments and everything else. It wasn't like that at all.
When I found out I was expecting I was up to my eyes in
my third year of organizing Miss UK, loving my job, and
with no thoughts of slowing down or – heaven forbid –
stopping work for quite some time. John was as thrown as
I was. We were used to doing what we wanted – working
hard, playing hard, having lovely holidays. Still, we were in
a brilliant position to have a child, even if it had caught us
off guard. John's business was doing well, I was earning
good money, and we had a lovely house with plenty of
room for a nursery. Just because we hadn't planned things
this way didn't mean we couldn't cope. I had been pregnant twice before, under very different circumstances.
This time, I knew straight away I wanted the baby.

I got onto the Miss World office and broke the news
to Eric Morley. 'I'm having a baby,' I said. 'It's due in
December.'

Eric wasn't exactly thrilled. He congratulated me and in
the same breath talked about me giving up work, as if that
was the only option.

It had never crossed my mind to stop working altogether and I told him I was keen to carry on running Miss UK for him. I was having the time of my life and I didn't want it to stop just like that.

'Angie, there's no way you'll want to keep working once you've had the baby,' Eric said.

'I will,' I said, determined. 'I'll take a bit of time off and then—'

Eric cut in. 'Your whole life changes.'

'I know, but—'

'I know what I'm talking about. It's going to be the toughest thing you ever do.'

He was adamant, and from the way he was talking I had a feeling my days running Miss UK were numbered.

All through my pregnancy I read as many baby books as I could get my hands on, wanting to know everything and be as prepared as I could. It never even occurred to me that there are some things you'll never be prepared for, no matter how many books you read. Every now and then I felt the odd flicker of panic at how much there was to think about. It was all so daunting and I had my moments when I wondered how I would ever cope with being a mother.

I worked up until September 1998 when Emmalene McLoughlin (related to Coleen Rooney) was crowned Miss UK. At that stage, I'd hardly put any weight on and most people couldn't even tell I was pregnant.

In the three months before the baby was due, when I was at home giving in to my craving for Thornton's chocolate fudge, I piled on weight. I'd always been slim so it was a struggle to come to terms with my new shape. I waddled about, feeling enormous. My ankles were swollen, my hands were swollen and I couldn't get comfortable in bed at night. The one thing that made me feel better was going for a swim every day at the pool down the road. The closer I came to giving birth, the more nervous I was. I kept ringing my mum for reassurance, but she was too honest for her own good.

'Does it hurt, Mum, you know, the actual giving birth?'

'It's the worst pain in the world,' she said. 'You'll never know anything like it.'

I was desperate for her to put my mind at rest, even if it meant telling the odd white lie. 'It's over quick, though, isn't it?'

'I don't know who told you that,' Mum said, 'but you can be in labour a long time. *Hours.*' She hesitated. 'Terrible pain,' she said. 'Terrible.'

A couple of weeks before the baby was due, my dad called round to see me. He had been to the market in Leicester and had bought loads of fruit. In the kitchen he heaved a bulging carrier bag onto the table, spilling out gleaming apples, red and green ones, firm yellow bananas, a net filled with satsumas, some big juicy oranges. It was the oranges I could smell. I started piling everything into the fruit bowl. There was enough to feed a small army, too much for John and me to get through.

'What's all this about?' I said, turning to fill the kettle.

Dad shrugged. 'I just thought I'd get you a bit of fruit.'

'You must have cleaned out the stall!'

He gave me an awkward smile and looked away. 'I've got something to tell you.' He hesitated. 'I've changed my name.'

The kettle started boiling and I switched it off. 'What do you mean, changed your name?'

'I'm called Sharif now.'

I laughed. Was this some kind of joke? His face was serious, though, and his shoulders shifted in another shrug.

I gazed at him. 'Why would you want to change your name?'

It was a while before he answered. 'I want to make Parveen happy,' he said at last.

Dad had been living with Parveen for something like five years. They seemed happy enough as they were and we all got along. I waited for Dad to say something else, to explain how changing his name from Ron could possibly make any difference. The next thing he said was that he had adopted Parveen's religion and converted to Islam. Until then, he had never so much as hinted that one day he might want to become a Muslim. I couldn't understand any of it.

Later, what haunted me wasn't so much what he said that day as what he didn't say. He didn't say he had come to say a last goodbye or that the fruit he had brought was his going-away gift. He didn't say he had no intention of meeting his unborn grandchild. He didn't say I would never see him again.

He just drank his tea and went.

I went into labour around two o'clock on the morning of 4 December 1998, and woke John. 'It's started,' I said. 'I'm having the baby.' We got a taxi to Leicester General, me hanging onto his hand, sweat running down the back of my neck, absolutely terrified. At the hospital, they put me in a wheelchair and took me up to the maternity unit. 'I'm having an epidural,' I told anyone who'd listen. If giving birth was as bad as my mum said I wasn't sure I could handle it. When the doctor arrived to give me the epidural I wondered if I'd made the right decision. The needle was massive, like an instrument of torture.

'Don't worry,' he said, all cheerful. 'It looks worse than it is.'

I had been lucky with my health and had never been in hospital for anything and I found it absolutely terrifying. I was convinced something would go wrong and kept telling John I didn't think I could deal with the pain. 'I think I'm going to die,' I kept saying.

'You're fine, Ange, they know what they're doing,' he said, trying to calm me down.

Joshua was born weighing 7lbs 9oz after a labour that lasted eleven and a half hours. As John had said, I was in good hands, and everything went without a hitch. Joshua was such a precious little bundle. I couldn't believe he'd been inside me. It didn't seem real and I cried my eyes out as I held him. John did, too. It was the most amazing feeling, just an overwhelming rush of love for this tiny person who was totally dependent on us for everything. I knew straight away nothing would ever be the same again. It had all changed in the space of a few hours.

Once I was home, just about everything I'd read during my pregnancy went out of the window. I'd had visions of creating a routine: Joshua sleeping in his nursery at the other end of the landing, having regular naps, me serenely breastfeeding. It was nothing like that. I felt totally unprepared and so protective I couldn't bear to let him out of my sight. For the first three months he slept in his Moses basket at the side of the bed and I constantly checked to make sure he was all right. I was determined to breastfeed but found it tough coping with the lack of sleep night after night, not daring to nod off in between feeds in case something happened to Joshua. I was so scared something would go wrong if I took my eyes off him for even five minutes. Perhaps I was over-anxious because of what had happened to my little brother Trevor, I don't know. In no time at all, I was completely drained.

When I lived with Paul, one year in the run up to Christmas I'd worked on the markets selling Aran jumpers for a guy he knew. It meant getting up in the dark, around 4 a.m., driving to London to set up the stall, and being in the cold on my feet selling all day. By the time I packed up and drove home I'd have been on the go for a good sixteen hours. I was paid £100 a day, which was good money then, but it was a killer. A few weeks of those early starts and bone-numbing cold were more than enough. I'd never known tiredness like it.

Not until I had Joshua, anyway.

I had stitches from giving birth and my whole body felt sore and battered. I was at home all day but didn't seem to have the time for anything, what with feeding and changing Joshua and all the paraphernalia that goes with having a baby. I felt zonked out and was often in my dressing gown until lunchtime or later. I remember someone calling round one day to see how I was getting on and being absolutely mortified because it was midday and I still wasn't showered or dressed and the house was a tip with baby stuff everywhere.

I tried calling my dad to tell him about his grandson but he never answered the phone. I wrote to him and got no reply. Time went by and I heard nothing.

For the first six weeks I didn't manage to get out of the house at all. I just couldn't get on top of things and was finding breastfeeding hard going. When I finally put Joshua in his pram and took him out for the first time it felt peculiar – the whole thing of pushing a pram and negotiating kerbs was completely alien. I had thought it would be so natural, but hadn't reckoned on how responsible I would feel for this little person and how stressful that would be. To start with, I only took him down the alley at the side of the house, round the block and home again. For the first six months or so I was really finding my feet.

Despite discovering that being a mother was much more challenging and difficult than I'd imagined, I had no doubt Joshua was the best thing that had ever happened to me. I doted on him. He was my world, the most precious thing in my life, and the love I had for him was like nothing I'd ever felt before.

I was loath to admit it, but Eric Morley had been right about my world being turned upside down. For the first few months after Joshua was born I was in no fit state to work. It was a struggle to get dressed in the mornings, let alone think straight or deal with the pressures of a demanding job. My head was all over the place. As time went on, though, I started to get my energy back and life at home settled into something of a routine. I was ready to take on something, as long as I could do it mainly from home and fit my work around Joshua.

One of the judges at the final in Blackpool of Miss UK 1998 had been John Dale, editor of *Take a Break* magazine. I knew he was interested in getting the magazine more involved. That year one of my colleagues, Mark Darlington, was hosting many of the regional Miss UK heats, and we decided to suggest to John we run a Miss Take a Break competition with the winner going through to Miss UK 1999. John could feature the winner on the cover of the magazine. He jumped at it. I gave him some editorial content and an entry form and within three weeks of it appearing in the magazine the entries had topped 5,500. Mark and I helped whittle them down to around 1,500, and then set up auditions in Leeds, Leicester and Guildford, with 500 to 600 girls at each one. The only way to get through so many girls in a day was to stick to a strict timetable. They came in and were photographed and interviewed, everybody getting the same amount of time so we kept things moving along. It was like a military operation. We ended up with an initial shortlist of forty appearing in the magazine and then, after a readers' vote, we got our final six. We ran the final in London and Nicola Willoughby from Lincolnshire took the crown. She was beautiful with amazing blue eyes, blonde hair and a perfect figure. She was training to be a paramedic and I think that, plus her looks and personality, impressed the judges. She went on to win Miss UK that year and took part in the Miss World competition at Olympia in London.

The following year the Miss World office decided to run separate beauty pageants for England, Northern Ireland, Scotland and Wales instead of a single Miss UK competition. I was on the sidelines, still running Miss

Leicester and Miss Nottingham, fitting my work round looking after Joshua.

It was in 2001 that I got a call from the Miss World office asking if I had any girls I could put forward for Miss England. I suggested Sally Kettle, who'd won Miss Leicester, and Katie Osbourne, who was Miss Nottingham. Sally won Miss England and Katie was runner-up. The following year, in 2002, I took the licence for Miss England.

Although my career was starting to get back on track my marriage was in trouble. John and I had somehow drifted apart and become more like best friends than husband and wife. There was no sudden falling out, nothing dramatic, more a gradual decline as our relationship shifted to a different footing. I wasn't sure exactly when things started to go wrong, although everything did change after Joshua was born. It's true what people say – having a child is a massive turning point. For those first few months I was oblivious to everything except the baby. Maybe there had been signs something was amiss between John and I and I hadn't picked them up. Or maybe I had and had simply chosen to ignore what was going on between us. At first it was as much as I could do to cope with being a mother. I didn't have much energy left for anything – or anyone – else. All that seemed to matter when Joshua was a baby was his well-being.

Whatever happened with John and me, neither of us wanted Joshua to suffer. His happiness was all that mattered. We decided to separate. I would never say that ending a marriage is an easy thing to do, but at the same time hanging onto something that's not working seems pointless. I know some people stay together because of their children, and that's fine if it works, but to me it made more sense to go our separate ways before Joshua was old enough to understand what was going on. That way, he would have two loving parents who got along well, even if they weren't together any more. John had helped get me back together after an abusive relationship had left me in bits and I was thankful to him for that. He had made me laugh and shown me that life was still worth living. And he was the father of my beautiful boy. John is a great dad. He adores his son. No matter what, I wanted us to stay friends and get along, for Joshua, and he felt the same.

51

The heat for Miss Merseyside 2002 was in the basement of a club in Liverpool called Garlands. A few hours before the event I was up to my eyes liaising with the club DJ about music, sorting out lighting, and running through choreography when the girls started arriving for rehearsals. My sister Becky, who was helping out, took a call from the mother of one of the girls who said there'd been some trouble and her daughter couldn't make it. The girl was Danielle Lloyd. I got on the phone to her mum to find out what was going on. It turned out Danielle's boyfriend was the jealous type and had kicked off about her taking part in the competition. Straight away, alarm bells rang and I thought back to Paul pushing me around and making me feel rubbish about myself. I had no way of knowing exactly what had gone on between Danielle and her boyfriend, but I didn't see why she should miss out on the competition.

I said, 'I'd love her to be here. She won her place in the final fair and square and it would be such a shame if she never got the chance to compete.'

'I know she'd still love to do it,' her mum said. 'I could have a word, see if she's up to it . . .'

'Tell her to come down. We'll look after her.'

When Danielle showed up she was covered in grazes and had clumps of hair missing. Her boyfriend's way of letting her know he didn't want her in a beauty pageant had been to drag her from a moving car and beat her up. At eighteen years old, Danielle came across as incredibly brave and strong. Although she was still shaky, she was determined to take part. Becky did her make-up and covered the marks on her face and Danielle went on stage. She held it together but I could tell how nervous she was parading down the catwalk in front of the judges. It was obvious her confidence had taken a severe knock and I could see nerves getting the better of her. No way was she going to be able to give her best that night. Even so, she was beautiful, natural and fresh-faced with lovely olive skin and clear hazel eyes. I admired her so much for getting up there and giving it a go after what she'd been through a few hours earlier. Although she wasn't placed, I took her to one side afterwards and encouraged her to do more competitions and get as much experience under her belt as she could. She reminded me so much of Vivienne, the girl who'd won Miss Hawaiian Tropic the year I'd made the final, and I said maybe she'd like to think about doing that next.

A few months later, I ran my first Miss England competition at the Liverpool Olympia. I had no sponsors, certainly no budget to do anything fancy with the venue, but at least I'd got that for free, and a simple star cloth at the back of the stage worked fine. Sally Kettle, the previous year's Miss England, hosted the event and I managed to get the reigning Miss World, Agbani Darego from Nigeria, on the judging panel. I wanted to make the contest a bit different so instead of a swimwear parade I put the girls in sportswear – leotards and leggings, that kind of thing. I did my best to get the press interested, but there was very little coverage. Beauty pageants were hardly front-page news, even if we did have Miss World there. I wondered what it would take to persuade them we were newsworthy. It wasn't long before I found out. The girl who won the title, Danielle Luan, was a student from Oxford Brookes University and she went on to represent England at the Miss World competition held in Nigeria the following November. Before the girls flew out, there had been some discussion about whether to hold the contest in Nigeria, because of a campaign protesting against the death sentence given to a young Nigerian woman. The campaigners were calling for a boycott of the competition. Some of the girls pulled out but Danielle went ahead.

A few days later, I was at home doing the ironing when I saw a newsflash on TV saying there was rioting in Nigeria over the Miss World pageant. As I stared at the television, shocked, the phone started ringing. It was Danielle's dad wanting to know what on earth was going on and whether his daughter was in danger. I wasn't sure what to say. I didn't know any more than he did at that stage. I got onto the Miss World office and they insisted the trouble was miles away from the capital, Abuja, where the girls were staying, although the news reports made it look as if there were violent protests going on right outside the hotel. What inflamed things was a story in one of Nigeria's daily papers, *Thisday*, suggesting the prophet Mohammed might have picked a Miss World contestant for his wife. The piece caused huge offence and a fatwa was issued against the journalist, a woman, who went into hiding.

Although I'd been assured the girls were in no danger,

Danielle's parents were worried sick. What had started as a brief newsflash was now headline news. It was alarming the way things escalated. I kept in touch with her parents, relaying news from Miss World, stressing the girls were all safe and secure. 'We just want her home,' her dad said, and I couldn't blame him. I was churned up, too, and felt horribly responsible for Danielle.

There had been protests against Miss World before – most famously when flour bombs were thrown at the compere, Bob Hope, at the Royal Albert Hall in 1970 – but nothing like this. In the space of a few days, more than 100 people died and another 500 were injured in the riots on the streets of Kaduna, north of Nigeria's capital city. Suddenly, from having no press interest, the papers were all over Danielle, and she was splashed across the front page of one of the Sunday tabloids under the headline 'Get Us Out'. Although the Nigerian authorities wanted the competition to go ahead there, in the end it was switched to Alexandra Palace in London. When the girls landed at Heathrow, Danielle was practically mobbed by photographers.

Certainly, once she was back in London safe and sound and I managed to speak to her, it was clear how harrowing the whole experience had been. For most of the girls who take part in Miss World it's the fulfilment of a dream, but for Danielle the whole thing became a bit of a nightmare.

The following year, Jackie Turner won Miss England at the old Hammersmith Palais in London and went on to compete in Miss World in China – thankfully, without incident.

*

In 2003 I was having a night out in Leicester with my sister Becky when I met Nigel. I think we got chatting because we were probably the oldest people in the club that night! Nigel had the same deep-set eyes as my first boyfriend, Mark, and when Becky saw him she did a double take. She actually thought it *was* Mark. Sometimes, in photographs I can see a resemblance but that's as far as it goes. Although Nigel was based in Cheltenham we started seeing each other and just seemed to get along. Both of us were strong-willed and fiery, so we didn't always see eye to eye but somehow the relationship worked. He proved a real help when it came to the pageants, driving me to events around the country, and pitching in to set things up.

He was with me at the Miss England final in Bournemouth in 2004, where there was a familiar face in the line-up. Danielle Lloyd, who'd competed for the Miss Merseyside title two years before, despite being beaten up by her boyfriend, was back, and it was as if she was a different girl. She had done what I suggested and entered Miss Hawaiian Tropic, won the title, and through that secured her place in the final of Miss England. It was hard to imagine the glowing girl who now shone on the catwalk, so poised and self-assured, was the same person who'd shown up in Liverpool covered in bruises with clumps of hair missing.

I was thrilled to see the transformation. She was a great candidate and I don't think anyone was in the least bit surprised when she won. At the party afterwards in the bar of the hotel where we were all staying, Danielle kept her sash and crown on and posed for snapshots with her boyfriend. As usual, I had struggled to get the press to cover the event but the *Sun* had promised a photo shoot with the winner the following day. Nigel was on stand-by to get Danielle to the studio. When he offered to drive her, her boyfriend said he'd be happy to do it.

'You don't mind driving to London?' Nigel said, knowing some people hate the capital.

'No, I don't mind driving at all,' the boyfriend said.

A few months later, Nigel spotted a photo in the paper of a young racing driver tipped for stardom. 'Isn't that Danielle's boyfriend?' he said.

I studied the picture. 'Yes, I'm sure that's him.'

Nigel grinned. 'Well no wonder he was happy to drive.'

Her boyfriend was the future Formula 1 champion, Lewis Hamilton.

As part of Danielle's Miss England reign I had arranged for her to do a cover shoot and an interview for *Take a Break* magazine. It seemed to me an opportunity for her to open up about the abusive relationship she had been in and by telling her story help other women. I was careful not to put pressure on her, knowing from my own experience that it wouldn't be an easy thing to talk about. I had struggled for years after getting away from Paul to tell people what had really gone on – partly out of embarrassment, and partly because it upset me to talk about it. Still, I knew Danielle was a strong character and that she could do a lot of good by speaking out. She was amazing, so open and honest about what she had been through, and it was a moving interview. I thought she was incredibly brave. Subsequently, she went on to work with a charity that helped women who had suffered domestic violence and, in 2009, she also made a powerful documentary, *Dangerous Love*, for Comic Relief, in which she spoke about her own experience.

52

In 2005, I took the Miss England contest back to Danielle's home town of Liverpool, to the Olympia again, and got her to host the event. On the judging panel was a girl she had become good friends with at the Miss World pageant in China – Miss Peru, Maria Julia Mantilla, who also happened to be the reigning Miss World.

I knew that the contest in 2005 was likely to have a higher profile than the ones I'd done before because we had four Muslim girls in the final and the press were already starting to jump up and down about it. What I didn't know was how frenzied the whole thing was about to become.

The day before the competition I arrived in Liverpool and headed straight to my hotel with Lisa Powell my choreographer, and Nigel. The Liner had just opened and we'd got a good deal on rooms for all the contestants, but when I pulled up at the entrance and saw the front covered in scaffolding my first thought was it wasn't even finished. Inside, though, everything had been done and it was lovely, and I started to relax. I'd only just got to my room when my phone started ringing.

'Is that Angie Beasley?'

'Yes, speaking.'

It was a journalist calling to ask if I knew about the threats to the competition from a Muslim cleric in Liverpool.

My heart started to beat a bit faster. 'I'm not aware of anything,' I said.

'It's just this cleric' – he said his name – 'is threatening to sabotage your event.'

I sank onto the bed.

The journalist went on, 'So, you say this is news to you?'

'I've not heard anything. Where did you get your information from?'

'We've been told by a very reliable source in Liverpool that your competition will be targeted by extremists.'

I felt sick. It wasn't very long since the 7 July bombings in London and everyone seemed to be on tenterhooks. I hung up and went down to the hotel lobby. I had no idea what to do next. I felt a stab of fear and it went through my mind that the safest option might be to pull the event. I had forty girls to think about and I couldn't afford to take any chances with their safety.

In the hotel reception, Hamdi, the promotions manager, came over to ask if I was settling in and looking forward to the competition.

'Well, I was, but I've just been told we're going to be targeted by protestors and I don't know what to do.'

'What – something serious?'

I told him what the journalist had said. 'But I know that cleric,' he said. 'I go to his mosque. Do you want me to see if I can find out what's going on?'

I had pulled out the stops to raise the profile of that year's final, getting Richard Quest from CNN on the judging panel, even persuading CNN to give us some coverage. A horrible thought dawned. Maybe the only reason they were interested was because they'd been tipped off there was going to be trouble. I got myself in a real panic thinking about all the things that could go wrong.

A few hours later, Hamdi got in touch. The cleric had no idea what he was talking about. 'He didn't even know Miss England was happening in Liverpool,' he said. 'He says you're not to worry.'

The next morning a national newspaper, one of the broadsheets, ran pictures of the four Muslim finalists and claimed there were threats of a fatwa against them. My phone was red hot with calls from the press and TV crews, all wanting to cover the event. My stomach was in knots. I still thought that maybe I should pull the plug on the whole thing. I went to a meeting of the management of the Liverpool Olympia, who insisted they had total faith in their security. I spoke to everybody on my team. They all agreed we should go ahead.

On the night, all eyes were on Miss Nottingham, Sarah Mendley, who'd spoken to the press about wanting to be the first Iraqi Muslim girl to wear the Miss England crown. Sarah was striking, tall and curvy, and every time she walked down the catwalk hundreds of flashbulbs went off. It was as if the press had already decided she had won and that the competition was just a formality. When it got down to the last seven there was another Muslim girl, Hammasa Kohistani, who had shone on stage. Instead of a swimwear parade we'd had a talent round and she had done an amazing belly-dance. She was fun and at the same time elegant and beautiful, one of those girls with natural poise and grace. The first time I'd set eyes on her was when she arrived at the venue in a smart little suit looking like a modern-day Audrey Hepburn. I was on the judging panel and by the end of the evening was in no doubt she deserved the crown. The press went mad and the next day she was all over the papers, on television, her picture wired around the world – the first Muslim girl to win Miss England. Despite all the fuss and fear beforehand, as Hamdi's cleric friend had promised, there wasn't so much as a hint of trouble during the event.

All night, I tossed and turned thinking about the photo shoot we'd arranged for the winner at Liverpool docks the following day. Miss England was due to face the press . . . in a swimsuit. I couldn't help thinking it was asking for trouble, bearing in mind Hammasa's beliefs. I think I was more uncomfortable with the idea than she was and we decided to compromise and cover her up with a sarong. It was the right decision. When we got to the location there were dozens of photographers and TV crews there, jostling and shouting. I had never seen anything like it. Hammasa took the whole thing in her stride, as if it was completely normal to be mobbed by snappers. When I found out a bit more about her, that her family had fled the Taliban in Afghanistan, and she had once dodged a bullet, it all made sense. A salivating press pack yelling to turn this way and that was tame by comparison.

In 2006 Miss World was held in Poland and I decided to go and support Miss England, Eleanor Glynn. Within a couple of weeks of being crowned, Eleanor had admitted she was terrified of flying and anxious about getting to Warsaw. We arranged for her to do one of Virgin Atlantic's Flying Without Fear courses which seemed to do the trick until the competition drew closer. Then she begged me to let her go by boat or coach or train . . . anything as long as she didn't have to get on a plane. I checked all the options but it would have taken too long to get her there. She was going to have to fly. At Heathrow, I braced myself for her to go to pieces when the time came to go through to departures but she was fine. Not a hint of worry. The Flying Without Fear course had done its job after all.

It was only when the competition was over that things took a turn for the worse. I had arranged to fly back to Luton with Eleanor and Nigel. On the night we were due to leave there was the most terrible storm and we waited in the airport departure lounge while thunder rumbled overhead and lightning lit up the sky. Rain lashed down. Eleanor was pale and I did my best to reassure her. 'There's no way they'll take off in this,' I said.

A few minutes later our flight was called.

We boarded and Nigel took the window seat, I sat beside him, with Eleanor in the aisle seat. She craned her neck to see what was going on outside. The rain on the tarmac was running in small rivers and lightning flashed overhead. She winced. 'Don't worry,' I said, seeing the panic in her eyes. 'They'll have to wait until it eases off.'

The captain's voice came over the public address system, smooth and authoritative. 'Good evening, ladies and gentlemen, we will shortly be preparing for takeoff . . .'

Eleanor dug her nails into my arm. 'I thought you said they wouldn't fly in this.'

'Well, I . . .'

She ducked her head in front of mine, straining to see what the weather was doing. If anything, it seemed to be getting worse.

'They'll only take off if they're sure it's safe,' I said.

Eleanor hung onto my arm. 'I've got a really bad feeling,' she said. Her eyes were wide, terrified. 'I don't think we're going to make it.'

I gave her what I hoped was a convincing smile. 'Eleanor, it's fine. I've flown loads of times and I've never had a bad experience.'

'I'm telling you, I can *feel* it. Something awful is going to happen.'

The man in the aisle seat opposite looked over. She was gripping my arm so hard I thought she might stop the circulation. 'Ssh, keep your voice down – you'll panic people.'

Her eyes were shiny. 'I'm panicking already! They've got to let me off.'

One of the cabin crew bustled over. 'There's nothing to worry about,' she said in the same smooth, authoritative tone the captain had used. 'Once we're airborne it will be fine, you'll see.'

I gave Eleanor a squeeze and prised her hand off my arm. I was wishing her parents weren't booked on a different flight back to Heathrow. I felt completely responsible. 'See, it's fine,' I said, no longer so sure of myself.

The flight was the worst I had ever been on with the plane tossed about in what felt like constant turbulence. Eleanor cried her eyes out. In between loud sobs she told me she knew we were going to die. I could see people watching and whispering about the hysterical girl in the aisle seat and I could feel her terror getting to me. As the plane lurched and shook I couldn't help wondering if she really had had some kind of premonition. We went through a series of stomach-churning drops that made me think of the Tower of Terror ride I'd been on in Florida. I looked at Nigel. Neither of us said anything but I had a pretty good idea he was thinking the same as I was: Are we going to be okay?

As we approached Luton, the captain announced that the south-east of England was gripped by severe weather conditions and we would have to join a queue for a landing slot. Eleanor gave me a pleading look. Through the window at the side of Nigel, we could see planes stacked up.

Her voice was small. 'We're not going to get down.'

The faces of the passengers around us were white and pinched with worry. Finally, we began our approach to the runway. Eleanor's eyes were shut tight and she had hold of my hand. I was thinking, Thank God, at last, just as the wheels of the plane hit the tarmac, bounced back up, and we soared into the air again. Eleanor was no longer the only one screaming. I grabbed Nigel's hand. There was no reassuring announcement from the flight deck, nothing, as we headed away from the airport before coming in to land again. Across from us I could see two guys who worked for Miss World, big burly blokes with their heads in their hands, praying out loud. Eleanor wailed. I didn't bother trying to shush her.

On the second attempt the plane landed safely and everybody on board clapped and cheered. I gave Eleanor's clammy hand a rub.

'It's not like that usually, honest it's not.' I managed to say although I could hardly get the words out I was so upset.

Her face was streaked with tears. 'I'm never getting on a plane again,' she said.

I didn't say anything because I knew exactly how she felt. It was a year before I got my nerve back and flew again.

53

I had first seen Rachel Christie in 2008 when she entered the Miss England competition that year. In 2009, she was back, competing in the final of Miss London at Movida nightclub in the heart of the West End.

Georgia Horsley, who won Miss England in 2007, hosted the night with Laura Coleman, the 2008 winner. Laura was seeing Danny Jones from McFly, who she'd met at Miss World in Johannesburg the year before, and he came along to support her, throwing his own little party in a cordoned-off VIP area.

I didn't know much about Rachel Christie. Nobody did. After she was crowned Miss London that night I sat down with her and asked if there was anything newsworthy we could tell the press, just something to ignite some interest, especially as Miss England was being held in the capital that year.

Rachel had a think. 'There's my uncle – he's Linford Christie,' she said.

My jaw dropped. '*The* Linford Christie – the *sprinter* Linford Christie?'

She nodded.

I was kicking myself. I knew Rachel was an athlete, in training for the heptathlon for the 2012 Olympic Games, but I just hadn't put two and two together. The competitions tend to be so hectic with so much going it's sometimes impossible to take in who all the girls are, and up until then Rachel had kept quiet about her famous relative. I set up an interview with the *London Evening Standard*. It turned out Rachel had an extraordinary story to tell. Hers had not been the easiest of upbringings. In 1996, when she was eight years old, her father, Russell – Linford's brother – had been stabbed to death in a row over drugs. Rachel was willing to talk about her dad's murder and how she had grown up determined to be a successful athlete, training at the stadium named after her uncle. She was a real inspiration.

In July 2009 Rachel arrived at the Hilton Hotel on London's Edgware Road for the Miss England final completely stressed out. She had been in an accident in her brother's car and ended up with whiplash and bruising. Once on the catwalk, though, her smile lit up the room and she dazzled. In the evening-wear parade she looked amazing in a white dress by the designer Karen Karmody. The judges, including Caprice, the actor Chris Fountain, Andrew Minarik who was head of hairdressing for Miss England and Laura Coleman – about to hand over her Miss England crown – were bowled over. The atmosphere in the venue was electric when twenty-year-old Rachel took the title. The runner-up, Katrina Hodge, a Lance Corporal in the British Army who'd been decorated for bravery in Iraq, caused quite a stir too.

The press interest was huge. Rachel was the first black Miss England and the following day she was interviewed live on ITN news. I stayed on in London to manage all the media attention. *Hello!* magazine set up an interview at the Royal Garden Hotel in Kensington and gave me a list of all the things Rachel would need for the photo shoot. When I ran through it with her she had none of the stuff they'd requested. She really had very little. Even the Karen Karmody dress she had worn on the catwalk was borrowed. I ran over to H&M on Kensington High Street and raced round the shop, buying up clothes and accessories, thinking the Miss England title with its £25,000 prize package including a holiday in Thailand, make-up, clothes and all kinds of things had gone to a thoroughly deserving winner.

I was convinced Rachel would do well in Miss World, especially as they had introduced a sports round to the competition, and in the months leading up to the final in South Africa, Caprice took her under her wing and coached her. The press interest never went away and every few days there'd be another story in one of the papers about Rachel. I knew she was struggling to get to assignments because she didn't have a car and persuaded Renault to sponsor her. When they arranged a presentation to hand over the keys to a black Renault Megane sports convertible she was in tears. From having very little, she was starting to enjoy a few nice things.

The Miss World competition loomed and I had arranged to pick Rachel up and take her to Heathrow Airport for her flight to Johannesburg on Thursday 5 November 2009. The Monday before when I got home after dropping Joshua off at school the phone started ringing. The woman on the other end said she was a police officer calling from Manchester. I couldn't understand why she wanted to speak to me.

'You're the only contact we've got for Rachel Christie,' she said.

'Rachel? She's Miss England. What's happened?'

'She needs to come into the station within the next twelve hours or she'll be arrested.'

'What on earth has she done?'

'Allegedly, she's assaulted somebody in a nightclub.'

I felt as if the breath had been punched out of me. 'Rachel? Are you talking about the same girl?' The Rachel I knew was gentle and mild-mannered. The call had to be a wind-up.

'The thing is,' the woman on the other end said, 'we've got a lot of press interest and they want to know what's going on, and when she's coming in.'

This was getting worse. 'How on earth do the press know about this?'

'So if you can pass the message on. As I say, if she fails to report in we'll arrest her.'

By the time I hung up my head was spinning. I tried calling Rachel and left a message. Eventually, she called me back. 'The police have been on the phone and they're saying you've got to go to the station in Manchester or they'll arrest you. It's to do with an assault,' I said, still hoping it was a horrible misunderstanding and that she would put my mind at rest.

Instead, she explained that the night before she had been at a party at the Mansion club in Manchester with her boyfriend and there had been some trouble with another girl. She then told me that a week or two earlier, when she'd been up north visiting him, all their stuff had been trashed by an ex-girlfriend of his.

I remembered her showing me a picture of her boyfriend, David McIntosh, also known as Tornado, one of the Gladiators. This wasn't sounding good. 'Why didn't you say anything about this before? And why did you go back up there when there'd already been trouble?'

'It was just a party and he asked me to go.'

My head was starting to bang. 'Rachel, you're going to the Miss World competition in a few days. You should be at home sorting out your stuff, getting some rest, not in some club in Manchester.'

I had no idea what to do. I rang my lawyer Gideon Cristofoli, who suggested I got a solicitor to go to the police station in Manchester later that day with Rachel. She was accused of punching Sara Beverley Jones, the reigning Miss Manchester, in a row over her Gladiator boyfriend, and was arrested on suspicion of assault and bailed for three months.

The whole thing was unprecedented and while I went round in circles trying to think up a solution, the papers were full of the alleged brawl. The *Sun* ran a picture supposedly showing Rachel and Sara in the club. I couldn't get my head round any of it. For one thing, the girl in the picture wasn't Rachel, and for another, how come a photographer from a national paper just happened to be in the right place at the right time? It didn't add up. Meanwhile, the Miss World office was on the phone, wanting to know what was going on and, in the face of all the bad publicity, the people from Renault who'd sponsored her car were getting twitchy.

On the day she was due to start the Miss World tour I went to pick her up from her granddad's house in London. I'd been on at her to come up with something for the competition's charitable Beauty With a Purpose round –

maybe get her uncle to sign something that could be auctioned to raise money. She came to the door clutching a rolled-up poster. 'I've got it!' she said. 'A signed photo.'

I felt dreadful. There had been no let-up from the press and I knew the whole Miss World dream was over for her. We packed her things into the car and set off, but instead of going to the Grosvenor House Hotel where all the Miss World contestants were I stopped at a hotel just down the road.

Rachel looked puzzled. 'What are we doing?'

My stomach was in knots. 'We just need to have a talk.'

We found a quiet corner and I said, 'Rachel, this is so difficult. You're supposed to be representing your country and you've been arrested on suspicion of assault. You're on bail.'

Her face fell.

'Do you have any idea how serious all this stuff is?'

She stared at the floor. 'Yes, course I do.'

'How can you enjoy being in Miss World with all this hanging over you?' I knew the press would hound her, that all the negative publicity would be destructive.

We talked it over, and could not see a way forward. We were both utterly devastated. In the end, we agreed she should step down as Miss England. It was the most painful conversation I've ever had; one of the hardest things I've had to do. Rachel was a lovely girl and I thought the world of her. She was beautiful, tall enough to be a catwalk model, and a hugely talented athlete. Without doubt, she would have shone at Miss World. I really thought she had every chance of winning the title and it was heartbreaking to see her dreams fall apart. The pair of us cried.

She didn't want to go home and face her family so I took her back to Leicester with me and she spent the night. Neither of us got much sleep and the next morning I took her to my gym thinking a workout might be a good thing, help bring the stress levels down a bit. Afterwards, she went to Manchester to be with her boyfriend. I then had to get on the phone to Katrina Hodge, her runner-up, to see if she could step in at short notice and go to Miss World. Katrina agreed and we ran through the list of things she needed to take: a long evening dress for the final, six to eight dresses (long and short) for evening wear, six smart day dresses or suits, a warm wrap for evenings, gold or silver high-heeled sandals, a tracksuit, jeans and T-shirts for rehearsals, a swimsuit/bikini with a sarong or wrap, trainers/shorts/sportswear. I shot back down to London and, between us, we got everything together in record time and off she went to Johannesburg.

For weeks afterwards, I couldn't sleep for worrying about Rachel. I thought about giving up the beauty-pageant business altogether and never organizing another Miss England competition. The whole thing had been so distressing. One episode in a nightclub was all it had taken to ruin things for Rachel. I did at least manage to persuade Renault to let her keep the car.

Around the same time, another story sprang up in the press, this one saying Danny Jones from McFly had dumped Miss England 2008, Laura Coleman, for her friend, Georgia Horsley, who'd won the title in 2007. I knew how keen Laura had been on Danny and thought back to the night in Movida when she had introduced him to Georgia. Looking back, it signalled the beginning of the end for her and Danny – and for her friendship with Georgia. It felt as if it was one thing after another, such a lot of heartbreak for girls I really cared about.

A couple of months later, in early 2010, all the charges against Rachel were dropped, but sadly Renault took the car because she had another court hearing about failing a breath test and they had had enough of the bad publicity.

54

It's a constant challenge to find ways to move Miss England forward and jettison the stereotypical image of bathing beauties in high heels. In 2010 we banned the swimwear round and there's now a Bootcamp element that puts the girls through their paces in a series of fitness challenges. I'm really passionate about the eco theme we came up with in 2007 that means at least one of the dresses the girls wear in the competition has to be second-hand – borrowed or maybe bought from a charity shop – or made from scratch using whatever recycled materials they can get their hands on. The idea is to even things out a bit, so that the wealthier girls who can afford to splash out on designer clothes are in more or less the same boat as the ones shopping on the high street. I'm in no doubt the whole eco theme stemmed from my never having new clothes when I was growing up and money being tight when I started competing in beauty pageants. Sometimes, I borrowed a dress or shopped around for a bargain, hoping nobody else turned up in the same outfit. I always knew which girls had money because their clothes stood out a mile.

Since the eco round was introduced to Miss England in 2007 it has injected some real character into things and become quite a talking point. In a sense, for me, it's as much about staying true to my roots as anything. I think it's a really positive message to send out. The girls can pretty much do what they want and some really let their imaginations run riot. In the final in 2010 one girl, Miss Rutland, Terri Anne Sutton, wore a dress made from CDs that shimmered as she went down the catwalk. Miss Durham, Alexandra Devine, made an elaborate outfit from her brother's Meccano set! Jessica Linley, who won the 2010 title, wore a simple off the shoulder peach dress that belonged to her mother. Anything goes.

Even now, I'm loath to spend ridiculous amounts on clothes and am always on the lookout for a bargain. I still rummage in charity shops and constantly recycle my best frocks – wearing the same thing for different events when I can get away with it. I never want girls to feel they can't take part in the competition because they don't have hundreds of pounds to spend on a dress.

I've always believed that beauty comes in different shapes and sizes. Some of the girls have the height to be catwalk models while others are very petite and don't conform to the strictures of the fashion industry. There's enormous pressure on young girls now to fit a particular ideal when it comes to beauty. You see it in the celebrity magazines all the time. Personally, I've never believed you have to be a size four to be beautiful and Chloe Marshall proved the point in 2008.

Chloe competed in the Miss Surrey contest. She was tall, very beautiful, and had a great personality. She was so full of beans she shone in the line-up with the other nine finalists and won the title. I had a photographer at the event and normally I'd have been glad to get some local press coverage, but the next day Chloe was on the front page of the *Daily Express*. She made everyone sit up and take notice because she was a size 16 and definitely not most people's idea of a typical beauty queen. Over the next few days Chloe featured in every tabloid newspaper and did a swimwear shoot that ran across several pages in *Hello!* magazine. Reading between the lines, it was obvious some of the press were having a dig because of her size, but she took it all in her stride. She projected such a fresh and positive image and in the Miss England final in 2008 was runner-up to Laura Coleman. She was subsequently signed up by the prestigious Ford Models agency in New York.

Chloe was exceptional and mostly girls taking part feel the pressure to be skinny. It's not unusual to see a girl lose a lot of weight after winning the title. I've seen two of my winners lose weight and within three months drop from a size 8–10 to a size 4–6. Suddenly, dresses that had been hand-made for Miss England for the Miss World final didn't fit any more and had to be altered. Of course, there are lots of naturally slim girls in the competition, but I never want to see anyone starve to conform to someone else's idea of beauty. Once or twice I've been really concerned when girls shrink and end up super-skinny and hollow-faced. If I think a girl goes too far and loses her sparkle, I'll definitely step in. To me, beauty is about being healthy and glowing, not stick-thin, which is why Miss England has supported Beat, a charity that helps people battling with eating disorders. I'd love to see more girls like Chloe Marshall take part in the competition because the message it sends out is so positive.

I do tend to feel protective towards the girls taking part in the competition and after what I went through when I was with Paul I'm always on the alert for signs of abusive relationships. I know when I see a possessive boyfriend. They'll turn up at venues and give the girl a hard time, make them cry sometimes. Mostly, the girls don't say anything because they're too embarrassed – which is how I used to feel when I was in the same boat – but if I think they're in trouble I'll have a quiet word and let them know they don't have to put up with any nonsense. I think it helps when I say I've been there. These days, I tend to come across as strong and confident and I can see how shocked people are when I say I experienced a huge amount of abuse, both verbal and physical. I wouldn't let anyone push me around now and I can't stand to see young girls go through it. Some girls won't admit what's going on, while others pour their hearts out. More than once I've comforted a girl who feels trapped by a violent boyfriend. It breaks my heart to think such confident, beautiful girls with so much going for them are being subjected to abuse. It's not something anyone has to put up with and deep down they know it.

Sometimes, they just need someone to remind them.

These last few months, working on this book, I've delved into bits of my past I thought I'd put away for good. Sometimes, I can't believe how much my life has changed since I first teetered along the catwalk as a shy teenager in the Miss Yorkshire Television heat in Cleethorpes thirty-odd years ago. As I got more confident and won a few titles, I discovered that being a beauty queen brought amazing opportunities. It was winning the Miss Leeds Metro title that landed me my dream job in a nightclub where I staged my first ever pageant, the forerunner to what I do today.

I'm still in contact with Terry George, the DJ who hosted the event with me. He went on to run Mr Gay UK and these days lives in a castle in Yorkshire and throws spectacular parties to raise funds for charity. Not so long ago he popped up on Channel 4's *The Secret Millionaire* programme, working undercover in a nursing home.

I'm as career-minded as ever, although there's no doubt my priorities have changed since having Joshua. He is number one, the best thing in my life, and I love him to pieces. I can't believe how proud he makes me. In December 2011 he'll turn thirteen and we're already talking about what he wants to do to celebrate. A ride in a stretch limo has been mentioned . . . When I was growing up, with my family not celebrating birthdays, I always felt the odd one out and I'd never want him to go through that. Since he was a baby I've thrown parties for him and made sure every birthday is a special occasion. He looks forward to it for weeks and on the actual day he's always up at some ridiculous hour wanting to open his presents. It's lovely.

I was never so bothered about missing out on Christmas. I didn't really mind not doing anything special, sitting down to egg and chips for dinner instead of turkey and stuffing, but these days I pull out all the stops for Joshua's sake and he absolutely loves it. If it wasn't for him I don't think I'd make much of it at all. I still think the Jehovah's Witnesses are right about a few things, and Christmas is one of them.

I've been with Nigel eight years now, and while things can be up and down between us I'm closer to him than I've ever been to anyone. I tell him everything and he's definitely good for me. He's like my dad and my boyfriend rolled into one! It's thanks to him I've started cycling again, something I'd not done since I was living in Grimsby. At the weekends, we ride along the canal towpath into Leicester and in the fresh air I can feel whatever might have got me stressed during the week melt away. Alternate weekends we're together as a family, the three of us, and then as a couple when Joshua is with his dad. John now has a daughter with his new partner so Joshua has a little sister and I couldn't be happier for him.

A huge sadness in my life is that my dad has never seen Joshua. I desperately wanted Josh to have a granddad, and I think my dad would have been brilliant. On New Year's Day 2000, just over a year after Josh was born, I did finally manage to get through to Dad on the phone. It's the only conversation we've had since that day in November 1998, towards the end of my pregnancy, when he arrived on my doorstep laden with fruit. My sister Becky was with me when I spoke to him and both of us were crying.

'I really want you to see Joshua,' I said.

'I'm sorry, I can't.' He was crying too.

'Why – why can't you?'

'I'm sorry.'

For reasons only he could explain, he had decided not to have anything more to do with his family. None of us have seen him or had any contact since that phone call. I don't know where he is living now. I don't even know if he is still alive.

As I write this, in April 2011, I'm flat out organizing the next Miss England pageant, and having the time of my life. I absolutely love it. The final is always hectic, two non-stop days. It doesn't matter how hard we rehearse or how well-drilled the girls are, things never go quite according to plan. One year, one of the mothers got a bit drunk and grabbed me by the throat when her daughter failed to make the final round. Another time I had an irate mother breathing down my neck when the video footage that accompanied the girls on the catwalk got out of sequence. Feelings can run high, but it's rare that we have a problem with any of the girls, even if one or two of the mothers sometimes go a bit over the top. I know from experience how disappointing it is to enter a pageant and not win, but you can't take it personally. Beauty is subjective and it all comes down to the judges on the night. A girl might enter one year and not get placed and then come back the following year and do really well.

This will be my tenth year as director of Miss England and I'm still as excited about everything as I was at my first national final in 2002 when it was a much smaller and less lavish event. I've built up a good network of regional organizers, many of whom have been with me for years now. It's brilliant for me to see how the competition has grown and developed and the calibre of girls it now attracts. Jessica Linley, who won the title in 2010, is studying to be a lawyer, Katrina Hodge, a serving soldier decorated for bravery in Iraq, wore the crown in 2009, and we've also had some impressive athletes competing. Miss Newark, Stephanie Pywell, who won our Miss England Sportswoman title in 2010, is also the British high-jump champion. They all work hard to raise money for the various charities we support. In 2010 we handed over a cheque for £109,000 to the Variety Club of Great Britain's children's charity.

I don't think there was ever a less likely beauty queen than me. When I was younger, I was so shy and lacking in self-confidence I never dared open my mouth. At school, I was always the quiet one in class. I hadn't a clue what I was doing the first time I got on the catwalk at the Winter Gardens in Cleethorpes, but it really didn't matter. The main thing was to get out there and give it my best shot. I knew it was a chance to make things better and I was determined to take it. I've no regrets because that one event led to so many opportunities. I don't think I fully appreciated it at the time, but my life changed course at that point. Through participating in and organizing beauty pageants, I have met and become true life-long friends with people I probably would have never crossed paths with if I had stayed in Grimsby working at the factory. Many are still involved with Miss England in some way or another.

I still believe that if you have a dream you have to go for it and not think too hard about whether you're good enough or what anybody else might say. It doesn't matter if you don't succeed right away. You can always have another go. None of us know what we can really achieve until we take a chance and, sometimes, one little act of courage doing the very last thing you'd ever think you were capable of – a few shaky steps along a catwalk in my case – can open the door to a whole new world.

He just wanted a decent book to read ...

Not too much to ask, is it? It was in 1935 when Allen Lane, Managing Director of Bodley Head Publishers, stood on a platform at Exeter railway station looking for something good to read on his journey back to London. His choice was limited to popular magazines and poor-quality paperbacks – the same choice faced every day by the vast majority of readers, few of whom could afford hardbacks. Lane's disappointment and subsequent anger at the range of books generally available led him to found a company – and change the world.

'We believed in the existence in this country of a vast reading public for intelligent books at a low price, and staked everything on it'
Sir Allen Lane, 1902–1970, founder of Penguin Books

The quality paperback had arrived – and not just in bookshops. Lane was adamant that his Penguins should appear in chain stores and tobacconists, and should cost no more than a packet of cigarettes.

Reading habits (and cigarette prices) have changed since 1935, but Penguin still believes in publishing the best books for everybody to enjoy. We still believe that good design costs no more than bad design, and we still believe that quality books published passionately and responsibly make the world a better place.

So wherever you see the little bird – whether it's on a piece of prize-winning literary fiction or a celebrity autobiography, political tour de force or historical masterpiece, a serial-killer thriller, reference book, world classic or a piece of pure escapism – you can bet that it represents the very best that the genre has to offer.

Whatever you like to read – trust Penguin.